Henri-Marie Boudon

The Hidden Life of Jesus

Salzwasser

Henri-Marie Boudon

The Hidden Life of Jesus

1. Auflage | ISBN: 978-3-84605-402-4

Erscheinungsort: Frankfurt, Deutschland

Erscheinungsjahr: 2020

Salzwasser Verlag GmbH

Reprint of the original, first published in 1869.

THE
HIDDEN LIFE OF JESUS:

A Lesson and Model to Christians.

TRANSLATED FROM THE FRENCH

OF

HENRI-MARIE BOUDON

ARCHDEACON OF EVREUX.

BY

EDWARD HEALY THOMPSON, M.A.

TO

THE MEMORY

OF

THE VERY REVEREND FATHER FABER,

PRIEST OF THE ORATORY OF ST. PHILIP NERI,

This Translation,

MADE AT HIS SUGGESTION AND WITH HIS ENCOURAGING APPROVAL,

IS INSCRIBED,

WITH AN AFFECTION WHICH DEATH HAS RENDERED SACRED,

IN GRATEFUL ACKNOWLEDGMENT OF

NUMEROUS AND GREAT BENEFITS CONFERRED

BY HIS WRITINGS, CONVERSATION, AND DIRECTION;

AND, NOT AMONG THE LEAST, BY

THE INTRODUCTION TO MANY SPIRITUAL AND DEVOTIONAL WORKS,

OF WHICH THIS PIOUS TREATISE OF

THE VENERABLE HENRI-MARIE BOUDON,

ARCHDEACON OF EVREUX,

IS NO UNWORTHY SAMPLE.

ADVERTISEMENT.

THIS little work, by the celebrated Archdeacon of Evreux, was selected by the late Father Faber to form one of the volumes of a series of Translations for Spiritual Reading which a zealous Catholic layman purposed undertaking some years ago, but of which only one volume, "The Spiritual Doctrine of Father Louis Lallemant," was actually issued.

The translator has been encouraged to venture on its publication by learning that M. Boudon's works were especial favourites with Mother Margaret, whose Life, just given to the world by her religious children, is sure, not only to engage much attention, but to leave its impress on the Catholic mind in this country. That holy woman had drunk deeply of the spirit of his teaching, and his writings exercised no little influence on her interior life; his book entitled *Dieu Seul* having "suggested" (as her biographers tell us) "the motto into which her whole spiritual system was compressed."

Boudon's works continue to be much read and highly appreciated in France. In some of them the keen eye of the theologian would detect certain inaccuracies of expression, which to the ordinary reader might not be perceptible, but which the author would certainly have corrected had he lived posterior to the condemnation of Quietism. From any such inadvertencies, however, the present treatise is perfectly exempt; and the divine who was appointed to examine it, previous to its publication in the year 1673, not only declared that it contained nothing in any way opposed to faith and morals, but pronounced the following high panegyric on its merits :—Its " holy teachings," he says, " will serve to perfect those Christians who shall either peruse them with attention or listen to them with devotion ; to confound the insolent presumption of the sinner, who offends God before His eyes, in His presence, nay in His very essence ; and to subdue the pride and vanity of men, who are enamoured only of the grandeur and applauses of earth, be their state, rank, or condition what it may, clerics or laics, when they read therein of the Hidden Life of Jesus, Son of the Eternal Father, Co-equal and Consubstantial with Him ; when they behold the hidden life of Mary, His holy Mother, the descendant of a line of kings ; of Joseph, her chaste and virginal spouse, of the same royal lineage ; of St. John Baptist, also of high extraction, who was sanctified in his mother's womb and declared the greatest of men by the sacred mouth of Truth Itself: all these holy personages having passed half of their life unknown to the world, that they might be known only to God the Father, the Holy Spirit, and the blessed angels."

The writings of this venerable man are remarkable for their simplicity and plainness: indeed, it may be inferred from what he says, that he purposely avoided all mere ornament of style and language lest he should divert the reader's attention from the subject and attract it to himself. His desire was ever to hide himself, to disappear from view, to be buried out of sight in the theme of which he wrote; if it were not rather that he was so entirely engrossed therewith that he gave never a thought to the words he used or to the mode in which he expressed himself. Hence a certain diffuseness and a habit of digression and repetition, natural in one who was possessed by an idea and allowed it to carry him whithersoever it would—who was desirous only of saying what was in his mind and careless of aught beside. Certain, at least, it is that Boudon studied none of the graces of composition, and paid little regard to its rules. The translator has made no attempt to elevate the style or to enrich the diction, a proceeding which, always unjustifiable, would have been especially so in the case of a work whose very object was to cast a slur, so to say, on all that bore even the semblance of ostentation and self-display. He has endeavoured, on the contrary, to retain, not only the unstudied plainness, but the peculiar phraseology of the writer, so as, if possible, to communicate to the reader something of the very taste and flavour of the work, though it were vain to imagine that any translation could preserve the freshness and fragrance of the original.

But, with all his disregard of literary excellence, Boudon's language is always forcible and pointed ; he never fails to leave a definite, nay a vivid impression on the mind ; and dull indeed of feeling must that soul be which is not touched and moved by the pathetic earnestness, rising at times to impassioned eloquence, with which in the present work he pleads the cause of God and reproaches men with their cowardice and indifference to His honour and interests ; and, again, the sad yet scathing irony with which he exposes the pride and self-assumption, not only of the worldly and irreligious, but of those who profess to lead, and even deceive themselves into supposing that they lead, a Christian life.

Yet in saying this we have said but little. No master of the interior life has exposed the pretexts and subtle artifices of self-love with more unrelenting rigour, or has tracked and pursued it, through all its doublings and turnings, to its last subterfuge in the hearts of those who love and serve God truly, but whom he would fain persuade to love and serve Him singly and perfectly, without evasion and without reserve. In all that Boudon writes there is one ever-recurring, predominant thought, one master-note that pervades, informs, and subjugates all else—God only.

Three biographies of the Archdeacon of Evreux have appeared in France, the last in 1837; but considerable materials remain in manuscript of which little or no use has yet been made. He died in 1702, at the age of 78.

An English life of this saintly man is still a desideratum, which it is hoped may be supplied ere long; but those who are not acquainted with his history ought to be informed that for eight years he lay under an imputation of a most disgraceful character, which he bore not only with patience but in silence, although it was the occasion of his being deprived for a time of his ecclesiastical office and being treated with general contempt. This period of his life has been—to use the author's own expression —dramatized, under the title of *La Folie de la Croix*, by M. Louis d'Appilly in one of those romance-biographies the only counterpart of which among ourselves is the historical novel. It was published at Paris in 1863.

The circumstance to which allusion has been made gives an affecting interest as well as a special significance to those passages in the present treatise in which the writer speaks of the blessedness of being afflicted, dishonoured, and abandoned here below, and so being enabled to enter more deeply into the hidden life of Jesus and made partaker in the choicest graces of His love. And here also it may be observed that Boudon covertly alludes to himself more than once in the course of this work:

as where (pp. 93, 94) he speaks of "a certain person" being favoured for a moment with a supernatural light which revealed to him something of the admirable marvels of the hidden life; and again where (pp. 135, 136) he describes how "a young man" resisted the urgent advice of his relatives, and even of his director, to sue for a benefice, and committed himself without reserve to the disposal of Divine Providence, which (he adds) had never ceased tending him like a gentle mother.

Some of the reproofs and exhortations which this zealous servant of God addresses to his contemporaries, ecclesiastics and religious, no less than laics and seculars, are happily not directly applicable to our days, seeing that the abuses incidental to lay patronage have long since disappeared—not to say that the Church has been everywhere stripped of her revenues and temporal dignities; but the spirit against which he inveighs—the spirit of worldliness —may be equally rife under any circumstances, and irreverence and profanity may be just as prevalent among ourselves, and just as offensive to the Majesty of God, although they may not exhibit themselves, in our churches, in the public and unblushing manner which Boudon describes. On the other hand, the whole argument of the book is eminently calculated to rebuke and put to shame that immodesty, audacity, and pretentiousness which is so characteristic of our own age, and which may insensibly affect even those who would seem to be furthest removed from its influences. As to impiety in the world at large, especially as directed against the Tremendous Mystery of the Altar, never—scarcely need it be said—was it more insolent or more malicious than now. By the more violent spirits Jesus hidden under the sacramental veils is hated with a hatred truly Satanic; while to the wise and learned of our generation He is simply an object of contempt—if it be not rather that He is so utterly despised as not to be deemed worthy even of such notice as contempt implies: He is not so much denied as ignored.

The dedications prefixed to the volume are so illustrative of the man and of his humble, tender piety that to omit them would have been an injustice both to author and to reader. They have therefore been rendered into English with, as far as possible, literal exactness.

E. H. T.

CHELTENHAM,

Corpus Christi, 1869.

CONTENTS.

PART I.

𝕵𝖊𝖘𝖚𝖘 𝖆 𝕳𝖎𝖉𝖉𝖊𝖓 𝕲𝖔𝖉.

CHAPTER I.

JESUS HIDDEN IN HIS GENERAL SELF-ANNIHILATION.

CHAPTER II.

JESUS HIDDEN AS TO HIS GENERATION—ETERNAL AND TEMPORAL.

CHAPTER III.

JESUS HIDDEN AS TO HIS NATURAL QUALITIES.

His natural gifts sublime, yet concealed. Father De Condren's answer when urged to write. The Gospels and their writers. Our Lord's teaching by parables a lesson to the learned and the intellectual. His concealment of His personal beauty a warning to the vain and self-complacent. His withdrawal of His sensible presence from His disciples contrasted with men's desire to display their natural advantages; and that even in the churches.

CHAPTER IV.

JESUS HIDDEN IN HIS PRIVATION OF TEMPORAL GOODS.

Jesus the King of kings, yet the poorest man on earth. Fruits of this poverty in the hearts of His followers. Advantages of compulsory over voluntary poverty. It admits to a deeper participation in the abject life of Jesus. Is more contemptible in the eyes of men. Devout people themselves ashamed of it .   .   .   .   .

CHAPTER V.

JESUS HIDDEN IN HIS PRIVATION OF THE ESTEEM AND FRIENDSHIP OF CREATURES.

Creatures engrossed with creatures. Desire of their esteem and approbation strong in us to the last. How nature predominates in the intercourse even of the good and devout. Jesus our model. His extreme and utter privations .   .   .   .

CHAPTER VI.

JESUS HIDDEN IN IGNOMINIES.

Nothing conceals more than contempt and disgrace. Loss of reputation a mark of God's love to us. A sure way of sharing the hidden life of Jesus. His treatment at the hands of men. Contrast of our pride and love of exaltation.

CHAPTER VII.

JESUS HIDDEN AS TO HIS POWER.

The ordinary conduct of Christians wholly opposed to that of Jesus. He who is All makes Himself nothing; and we who are nothing are always desiring to be something.

CHAPTER VIII.

JESUS HIDDEN AS TO HIS OFFICES AND DIGNITIES.

CHAPTER IX.

JESUS HIDDEN AS TO HIS GRACES.

CHAPTER X.

JESUS HIDDEN AS TO HIS DIVINE MISSION.

CHAPTER XI.

JESUS HIDDEN EVEN WHEN MOST SEEN.

His predilection for the hidden life; as shown in His conduct on Mount Thabor. His preaching rejected with scorn. The lesson this gives to those who desire the esteem of men. Jesus everywhere contemned and ill-treated.

CHAPTER XII.

JESUS HIDDEN IN HIS GLORIOUS LIFE.

The creature disputes pre-eminence with its Creator. Men are ever seeking to be noticed. The self-annihilation of Jesus in the Blessed Sacrament. His presence denied by heretics. Irreverence in churches.

CHAPTER XIII.

JESUS HIDDEN IN HIS MOST HOLY MOTHER AND HIS SAINTS.

How He humiliates Himself in everything that concerns or belongs to Him; while creatures exalt themselves. Profanations in domestic chapels. Jesus despised on account of the poverty of Mary and Joseph. The pride of birth. Jesus hidden in His religion. How few appreciate His holiest maxims. People ashamed of being devout. What devotion is in itself. In what the practice of devotion consists. The indifference and cowardice of men in God's behalf. Ridicule of devotion the height of folly. The failings of the devout no disparagement to devotion. Jesus hidden in His servants.

PART II.

Practice of the Hidden Life.

CHAPTER I.

THE HIGH ESTEEM WE OUGHT TO HAVE OF THE HIDDEN LIFE.

CHAPTER II.

WE OUGHT TO GIVE OUR AFFECTIONS TO THE HIDDEN LIFE WITH COURAGE AND FIDELITY.

CHAPTER III.

WE OUGHT TO COMBAT IN A CHRISTIAN WAY THE INCLINATION WE HAVE TO SELF-DISPLAY.

CHAPTER IV.

WE OUGHT CAREFULLY TO AVOID EVERYTHING THAT CAN MINISTER TO SELF-DISPLAY.

CHAPTER V.

WE OUGHT TO OBSERVE A CONSTANT WATCHFULNESS OVER OURSELVES BY THE FAITHFUL PRACTICE OF MORTIFICATION IN THOSE SITUATIONS WHEREIN BY THE PROVIDENCE OF GOD WE ARE OBLIGED TO PUT OURSELVES FORWARD.

CHAPTER VI.

WE OUGHT TO PRACTISE MUCH SELF-HUMILIATION, AND ENDURE WITH RELUCTANCE THE ESTEEM AND FRIENDSHIP OF CREATURES.

CHAPTER VII.

WE OUGHT TO REJOICE GREATLY IN BEING UNKNOWN.

CHAPTER VIII.

WE OUGHT TO MAKE A HOLY USE OF THE INTERIOR SUFFERINGS WHICH HIDE US FROM OURSELVES.

CHAPTER IX.

WE OUGHT TO LIVE AS IF THERE WERE BUT GOD ONLY
AND OURSELVES IN THE WORLD.

God the great All, and everything else nothing. This truth
little realized. The miserable consequences of this; even
amongst the spiritually-minded. The necessity of giving
heed to the light of pure faith. The illuminations it
produces in the soul. A soul so enlightened refuses all
satisfactions to self-love even of the holiest kind. Our
Lord's withdrawal of His sensible presence from His
Apostles. The most effectual means of detachment, to
live as if there were but God and ourselves in the world.
The blessed effects of this. The vanity of all created
things . . . . *page* 171

CHAPTER X.

WE OUGHT TO HAVE A SPECIAL DEVOTION TO THE HOLY
FAMILY OF OUR LORD, TO THE HOLY ANGELS, AND TO
ALL THOSE SAINTS WHO HAVE BEEN ESPECIALLY CON-
NECTED WITH THE HIDDEN LIFE OF THE ADORABLE
SAVIOUR.

Mary and Joseph the creatures most loved by Jesus; and
them it is He calls to share most largely in the privations
of His hidden life. How completely Mary hid herself, her
virtues, and her prerogatives from the knowledge and
esteem of men. The life of St. Joseph, how little known.
Our Lord seems to delight in withdrawing him from view.
The devotion due to St. John the Baptist, and other saints
who led a solitary life, or who were despised and ill-
treated by the world. They who are devout to the Hidden
Life ought to have a special devotion to the holy angels
who ministered thereto. . . . . *page* 180

TO THE

MOST HOLY VIRGIN,

HIDDEN WITH

THE ADORABLE JESUS

AND

THE GLORIOUS ST. JOSEPH

IN THE HOLY HOUSE OF NAZARETH.

MOST HOLY VIRGIN—

THIS little work, as well as all the others which
it has pleased thy Beloved Son and thee to give
me grace to write, I lay at thy feet; for to thee it is
due, and to thee it belongs by every kind of right.
Yes, I will repeat it everywhere, and I will say it
with inconceivable joy of heart: sweet it is to say it
again and again, and fain would I go on repeating it
for ever. Let the wise and prudent of this world,
those human philosophers, take occasion to carp as
much as they please, I will ever account it my
honour, an honour to be preferred before all the
sceptres and crowns of earth, to be thy servant, O my
Sovereign Lady. So long as I shall have the aid of
thy powerful protection, I will not be ashamed boldly
to confess it before men. By God's help, I will
declare it in private and in public; I will proclaim
it before all the world; I will write and I will speak
of it before men and angels; I will announce it in
the face of heaven and of earth; I will repeat it all

through my life and at my death. O my amiable*
Mistress, and most honoured Queen, grant, I humbly
beseech thee by the Heart of Jesus, by thine own
virginal heart, by all the nine choirs of angels and
the saints, grant that after my death I may still
repeat it for ever and ever, through a long and
endless eternity. O my glorious Lady, behold thy
poor servant always at thy feet, with all the little
works he has composed, and all other good actions he
may, by the divine assistance, perform : all are thine,
entirely thine.

But as the present work breathes only the love of
the hidden life, it is most meet that I should consecrate it to the honour of thine, which was all
hidden with the Most Amiable Jesus, thy Son, and
thy pure spouse St. Joseph. Incomparable Virgin,
admirable Mother of God, the sacred writers record
scarcely anything of thy greatness and divine perfections. There was found, indeed, a sacred historian
to leave to posterity the Acts of the Apostles ; and
through the course of ages there will be ever found
holy pens to publish the actions of the saints, often
even to the slightest and minutest circumstance,
disclosing to the eyes of the faithful the secret details
of their daily life. But as to thee, O most holy of
saints, the details of thy immaculate life remain
hidden from all the world. Ah ! it is because mankind are not worthy of them; the knowledge of thy
all-heavenly life is reserved for heaven. As the imperfections of earth had no part in it, the splendours
of its purity, surpassing even the purity of the angels,

* "Amiable" is one of those words which have come to
bear in common parlance a lower and shallower meaning than
primarily belongs to them. It is, of course, only the English
rendering of the Latin *amabilis*, with the devotional use of
which Catholics are familiar enough, as signifying, not only
"dear" and "lovable," but "worthy of love"—"worthy of
all love." With this its higher and deeper signification we
cannot afford to part, if only for the reason that the English
language contains no other equivalent.

belong more fitly to Paradise, the land of true light, than to this earth of ours, which is a region of shadows and of darkness.

I also dedicate this little treatise to him who, next to thee, O my kind, my faithful Lady and Mistress, is the most hidden of all pure creatures, the great St. Joseph, thy virginal spouse. O blessed saint, thou art blessed among all men for thy celestial union with the Queen of angels and of men, and by the precious title thou didst bear of the reputed father, the foster-father, of Jesus, Creator of heaven and earth, true God, in whose presence the powers of heaven tremble and the Seraphim veil their faces in reverence and love.

But before all, and above all, I offer it to Thee, I dedicate and consecrate it to Thee, O Adorable Jesus, by whose merits the Most Holy Virgin, St. Joseph, and all the saints have been sanctified and exalted so blessedly to the ineffable glory they enjoy. I consecrate it, with the deepest adoration, with the profoundest self-annihilation, with all conceivable gratitude to Thy life so divinely hidden, on this earth of ours, in the House of Nazareth, with Thy Mother ever immaculate, even from the first moment of her all-holy conception, and with St. Joseph, Thy amiable foster-father. Ah! fain would I for the rest of my days, and, if Thou wilt show mercy to me, for all eternity, honour, bless, praise, and love a life so hidden, which shall be for ever the object of the praises, the admiration, and the adoring love of Paradise.

Accept, O Holy Family, this little work, as a token of my most earnest desire to honour eternally Thy hidden life, and that it should be for ever honoured by angels, and saints, and all mankind. O ye angels of heaven, come to the aid of my desires; and you especially who were associated with the hidden life of this Most Holy Family, by your ministering care and the peculiar devotion with which you honoured it. O ye men and women, saints of Paradise, come to the aid of my heart's desires, and you especially who shared in a particular manner this hidden life: O great Saint John the Baptist, and thou, O amiable Saint John the Evangelist, so hidden, not only in thine exile in the Isle of Patmos, but also by thy crosses, so hidden in thy life, and still more hidden in thy death and after thy death'; blessed Saint Paul the Hermit, blessed Saint Onuphrius, glorious Saint John Calybite, glorious Saint Alexis, and thou seraphic Saint Teresa—all of whom I have chosen to honour, together with the holy angels, as the saints of my particular devotion —I pray you, for the glory of our common Lord and Master, to grant me your most powerful intercession with His Divine Majesty, that the hidden life of Jesus, Mary, and Joseph may be more than ever venerated by all the faithful; that it may be truly praised and loved by all mankind, through the destruction of all schism, heresy, and unbelief; that it may be worthily established in all hearts by a faithful expression and true imitation, and particularly in mine; all hearts emptying themselves of all that is not God, by a complete disengagement from every created being, no longer desiring anything but God only, no longer loving anything but God only, no longer attaching themselves to anything but God only. Ah! God only, God only, God only, for ever. Amen. Amen. Amen.

TO THE

HOLY BISHOPS

OF THE

DIOCESE OF EVREUX.

GREAT SAINTS—

MOST meet it is that, having paid my accustomed homage to my amiable Queen, by the dedication to her of this work, which I consecrate to her glory in honour of the Most Holy and Most Adorable Trinity, the Supreme End of all things, I should turn and prostrate myself at your feet, to offer and dedicate it also to you with that deep veneration which your greatness merits, and with all the submission, all the zeal of which I am capable, according to the grace I have received, for your honour and glory. Many motives, O glorious Pontiffs of Jesus Christ, constrain me to render you this testimony of my respect. I owe it to you as the Apostles of the Holy Gospel in the place where by virtue of my office of archdeacon I am bound to preach it in the course of my visitations. I owe it to you as the holy Bishops of a diocese into which Providence alone, my tender mother, brought me by ways known only to her—ways which I ought to adore, bless, and love eternally. I owe it to you as the fathers of the people who here live under the laws of Christianity, and whom you begot to Jesus Christ by your words and example; as faithful advocates, who, by your prayers and intercessions, maintain their interests before the throne of the Divine Majesty; as their mighty protectors, who defend them with such power against their enemies, visible and invisible. I owe it for inexpressible obligations by which I am personally bound to you. But further, this work on the "Hidden Life" ought most justly to be inscribed to you, because your invaluable lives were but one continual death to the present world, wherein buried, as it were, with our Adorable Saviour, you became hidden men, sacred men whom the world knew not.

O great St. Taurinus,* the world of Evreux knew thee not, seeing that when thou camest bearing the true light to this people, who sat in darkness and the shadow of death, they loved their darkness better than the fair dawn of grace and heavenly truth which thou didst manifest unto them, and treated thee as a false prophet and a deceiver. Man of God, the world of Evreux knew thee not, seeing that, all corrupted with the malignity of sin and sick even unto death, it regarded thy divine remedies as a hurtful poison; and whilst thou wert labouring with all thy strength to obtain for it true light, it bent all its efforts to compass thy death. O Apostolic man, thy loving heart had nothing for this world but inexpressible charity, while for thee it had but scourges, crosses, and exceeding torments.

Glorious prelate, thy life was hid with Christ in God, by thy disengagement from earthly goods, forsaking them to embrace a rigorous poverty which made thee the laughing-stock of the children of men; by the abandonment of worldly honours and the choice of an abject life, for which thou wert accounted as the offscouring of the earth; and by banishing thyself from thy native place, where men knew thee to be of noble birth. But a life so divinely hidden, the object of thy most ardent desires from thy tenderest

---

* Boudon wrote a life of St. Taurinus, which was published at Rouen, in 1694.

years—a life withdrawn from the gaze of all who might perceive thy eminent virtues—attracted to thee the favourable eyes of God, who so much the more regardeth those who do Him service, as they are the more careful to escape the notice of creatures. This generous contempt of the esteem and friendship of creatures it was that became in thee one of the most fruitful sources of the sacred graces and benedictions of heaven.

Men opposed thy teaching, for they could not relish that which was so adverse to their inclinations. The priests of the false deities persecuted thee, for thou didst break down their altars, destroy their temples, and burn the groves that sheltered their sacrilegious rites. The magicians sought thy life, for thou didst bring to nought their divinations. Hell conspired against thee, for thou laidst bare the malice and the wiles of the devils, and settest free the souls that groaned under their cruel tyranny. But whilst men weary themselves with smiting and scourging thee, confine thee in dark dungeons, and pursue thee to put thee to death, thy admirable patience amidst such great torments and ignominies wins from the almighty hand of God their entire conversion. The idolatrous governor who presided over the town of Evreux, his wife, and his son whom thou hadst raised to life, embrace the Christian faith. Multitudes renounce their Pagan superstitions. The very priests of the false gods and the magicians own the empire of the Adorable Jesus, and behold! well-nigh a whole infidel country is converted to God.

In vain, great saint, do the demons strive their utmost to oppose such glorious conquests; their craft and their rage serve only as occasions for thy most brilliant exploits; and these unhappy spirits are compelled to confess themselves thy captives, bound at thy feet by chains of fire, inflicting on them new and frightful torments. Do they appear in hideous forms at the gate of the town of Evreux, and attempt in vain to prevent thy entrance, by the power of God thou compellest them to assume shapes still more dreadful before the eyes of the people, in order to expel them from the place; and this thou effectest by the baptism of two thousand persons, who abandon their infidelity at the mere sight of those horrible monsters.

But whilst thou puttest to flight the demons of hell, thou admittest in their place the angels of heaven, and exaltest with their aid the glory of the holy cross; thou establishest the *cultus* of the admirable Mother of God, transforming the profane temple of the false goddess Diana into a holy church dedicated to the true God, under the invocation of the Blessed Virgin, whom henceforth thou gavest to the diocese of Evreux to be its patroness and protectress. Meet, indeed, was it that for so many holy actions of a life so separated from men, so hidden from the world, an angel from heaven should show thee under the form of a lily to thy mother before thy birth. They merited for thee the sweet protection of these blessed spirits during the whole course of thy pure life; and that at death these sublime intelligences should visit thee with their hands full of the transporting consolations of Paradise; and after death that these spirits, who are all love, should honour thy sacred tomb with strains of heavenly music, that men on earth might learn, by these sweet canticles to thy praise, the esteem that heaven hath of thy surpassing glory and admirable virtues.

O glorious St. Gaudentius, thy life was hid with Christ in God, not only by that exceeding height of grace and sanctity to which thou wert exalted, and thy interior saintliness, which things the world knoweth not, but also by thy voluntary retreat into a desert on the sea-shore, quitting the lofty functions of the Episcopate to lead the solitary life of a poor hermit in complete separation from earthly creatures. But the All-Good God, who takes care to make known those who hide themselves for His love's sake, seems to delight, O saintly man, in unveiling thy glory before the world, not only immediately after thy death, which commonly happens to most saints, but also through the course of ages, wherein His Providence ceases not to spread abroad thy fame, because during thy whole life thou labouredst without ceasing to conceal thyself.   Five hundred years after thy death did the All-Good and All-Merciful God publish thy greatness to the world, by the discovery of thy sacred body, which then was found incorrupt, and by numerous miracles which He wrought to honour thee.   And again in our time, only ten years ago (I write this in the year 1674), hath He rendered thee famous by a second invention of thy sacred relics, more than five hundred years after the first ; and this last invention, like the former, was honoured by several miracles, shedding a glory over thy sepulchre, hard by St. Michael's Mount in Normandy, chosen refuge of all who come to implore thy intercession. The graces which I there received, after the aid thou hadst rendered me in a mortal sickness, constrain me to publish everywhere that thou art the saint who helpeth in urgent need, and inspire me with a feeling of gratitude which I pray may endure as long as Eternity itself.   O heavenly man, I marvel not that thou obtainest so many favours for those who visit thy sacred tomb, seeing that from thy earliest youth it was one of thy pious practices to go and pay homage at the sepulchre of the great St. Taurinus. In that holy spot it was that thou offeredst continual prayers to the Divine Majesty, that it might please Him to give a holy bishop to the diocese of Evreux, deprived at that hour of its prelate ; thyself, by a loving Providence, destined to be that same holy bishop for whom thou prayest, though at the time thou knewest not the designs of God in thy regard.

Illustrious martyr of Jesus Christ, St. Eternus, thy life was hid with Christ in God ; and rarely was a life more hidden. The world is not worthy of it, the eyes of men are too feeble to endure its vivid, dazzling brightness, their understandings too gross to apprehend its sublime perfection. Thy witness is in heaven; thou soughtest but the eye of God alone, God alone sufficed thee; and when He had honoured thee with the crown of martyrdom, He exalted thee to His kingdom, where He made thee glorious in the midst of all the heavenly court.

Blessed St. Aquiline, thy life was hid with Christ in God, seeing that God alone was the paramount object of all thy thoughts, the exclusive occupation of thy heart; and so free wert thou from human respect and regard to creatures, for all acquaintance with which thou hadst a holy contempt, that, the more completely to forget them, thou didst beg from God the loss of sight, and didst obtain the boon thou askedst. Nay, was it not the love of the hidden life which led thee to erect a little cell outside the walls of Evreux, that there thou mightest lead a life separate from creatures, and be free to converse with God alone? In this sacred retreat it was that thou drewest down heaven's choicest blessings on the people of thy diocese, who, as the Acts of thy Life relate, felt themselves the more strengthened to put away sin and advance in the ways of God, in proportion as thou devotedst thyself more perfectly to the hidden life. Thy fervent prayers, the sighs and tears thou sheddest for their salvation before the Divine Majesty, shielding thy diocese as with an invincible defence, were to it an impregnable fortress, whereon hung, as on the tower of David, a thousand bucklers and all the armour of valiant men.

Angelic St. Laudius, thy life was hid with Christ in God. This hidden life it was that formed thy dear delight. Thou lovedst it with an affection so sweet and strong that, it may be said, never did an ambitious man so eagerly desire to be distinguished before the world as thou to be unknown. This desire, the gift of the Holy Spirit, made thee choose for thy dwelling a solitary cave, a league and a half from the town of Evreux, when thou wert canon of that church. In this forlorn cave didst thou live in straitest poverty, the hard ground thy bed and a stone thy pillow. Thy holy vigils lasted through the silence of the night; thy fastings and austerities were extreme, thy prayer continual, thy love for retirement so strong, that never didst thou quit thy beloved cave save only to recite the divine office in the cathedral church. But God, who draws nigh to those who forsake the creature, filled thee with His divine presence. Thou didst retire apart from men of the earth, and the angels of heaven bore thee company. Thou forsookest the charm of all worldly converse, and the celestial spirits cheered thee with the songs of Paradise. Thou desiredst to hear no news of this world, and heaven disclosed to thee its secrets. Thou renouncedst all honours here below, and God distinguished thee with His most signal favours. He was pleased to reveal to thee the glorious sepulchre of St. Taurinus, first Bishop of Evreux, by a column of fire which reached from earth to heaven, and vouchsafed that thou shouldst hear his praises chanted by angelic choirs. He chose thee to be one of his successors in the Episcopate, despite all the repugnances thou hadst for a dignity which would bring thee before the eyes of men.

O glorious confessors of Jesus Christ, O holy pontiffs, men of compassion, receive, according to the largeness of your great charity, the offering I make you of this little work, prostrate at your feet in all humility. Receive it as a testimony of my gratitude for all your goodness, as a token of my veneration, devotion, and zeal for your glory. I pray our common Lord and Master to establish and increase that glory more and more, and especially in this diocese of Evreux, that it may render to you who are its fathers a devotion truly filial. Great saints, how happy should I deem myself if, in the power of the same Lord and Master, I could contribute in any way thereto. But anywise, look favourably from the height of heaven on this diocese, which you governed with so much love and care. Deliver it, by your powerful intercessions, from the snares of its enemies; defend it against their assaults, and maintain in it the faith you preached, loyal submission to the Sovereign Pontiff, and devotion to the most pure and ever-immaculate Virgin-Mother, the blessed angels, and the saints. Preserve it from heresies and every kind of error; obtain abundant benedictions for all the prelates who shall succeed you here, and in particular for him who is now its most worthy father and pastor. O holy bishops of this diocese, powerful intercessors with the most high God, pray Him to increase the pure faith of this great prelate ever more and more; his fervent devotion to the admirable Mother of God, and especially in her Immaculate Conception; his eminent piety towards all holy things, his earnest zeal in defence of the Holy Apostolic See, and the destruction of every form of error. Pray for the clergy and religious, and, in your mercy, remember me, most wretched and unworthy. I beg your holy blessing for myself and for my office. Bless the archdeacon of Evreux, who seeks your aid with a confidence far greater than he can find words to express. Bless his archdeaconry, banish from it whatever hinders the glory of our Lord and of His holy Mother; subdue every hostility, visible and invisible, that may be raised against the cause of God. Establish in every part a truly Christian unity, the holy peace of Jesus and Mary, that the Name of God may everywhere be hallowed; His kingdom come, and that of His glorious Mother, as within the limits of this charge, so also throughout the rest of the habitable world; His will be done on earth as it is in heaven; and the cause of God only triumph everywhere for ever. Amen. Amen. Amen. God Only.

PART I.
JESUS A HIDDEN GOD.

CHAPTER I.

To name Jesus is to name a Man-God : but in whatever aspect we regard Him, whether we contemplate
His Divinity or consider His Sacred Humanity, we
cannot but say that Jesus is hidden.   If we consider
Him as He is God, may we not assert most justly
that He is in truth a hidden God, seeing that men
know Him not ; or, if they know Him, it is in a
manner so feeble and so strange that we may say that,
knowing Him, they know him not ?   Wretched we,
who live in a land of darkness and in the shadow of
death ! The Creator of all things is not known by
His creatures ; the world knew not Him who made
it.   How many ages rolled away in utter ignorance
of the Divinity, men of their own will darkening
their hearts by their own malice.   " In Judea is God
known," says the Psalmist (lxxv. 1), and the rest of the
whole habitable world, speaking generally, knew Him
not.   Even Judea had its darkness, its people being
prone to run into unbelief and idolatry.   But since
the bright day of grace has dawned, what multitudes
still remain in the blackness of unbelief ! How
many vast empires, kingdoms, nations, live in
ignorance of the true God !

And yet He is "not far from every one of us,"
says the great Apostle (Acts xvii. 27, 28); "for in
Him we live, and move, and be : " the God of Infinite
Majesty is everywhere, and He is everywhere with
all His beauty and perfections.   Let us go, O my
soul, from city to city, from province to province,
from kingdom to kingdom—let us go in spirit from
one end of the earth to the other—and we shall
behold all this vast world filled with the Infinite
Majesty of God, who is present in the smallest of
His works, in the minutest atoms ; for there is
nothing in which God is not, and where He is not
wholly what He is—the Three Divine Persons, the
Father begetting the Son, the Father and the Son
producing the Holy Spirit. We shall behold this
God present in all His creatures, preserving to them
the being they have received from Him, communi-
cating life and power to all that lives and acts. We
shall behold all creatures moving before the Divine
Essence, in the Infinite Being of God, who encompasses them around and replenishes them on every
side.   But shall we not behold well-nigh all creatures
steeped in a profound forgetfulness of this God so
infinitely adorable ? To believe that God sees us,
surely is enough to inspire all mankind with reverential awe in His Divine Presence. But to know,
without possibility of doubt, that not only does He
keep His adorable eyes fixed upon us, but that we are
wholly immersed in His Divinity ; and after this, not
to see Him, but to forget Him—this it is which is
incomprehensible. A servant of God, entering a
large city, in the company of many persons who
occupied themselves, as men usually do, with the
grandeur and beauty of the magnificent buildings

that met their eyes, was deeply touched with a vivid and tender perception that was given him of the little attention that creatures pay to the Presence of God. "See," said he, "how a mere mass of stones and such-like things occupy the thoughts of men and form the theme of their conversation, while the Infinite Majesty of a God is far more present to them than anything their eyes behold, and yet it is the only subject of which they never think!" Strange, but true. Go into the streets of some great city, repair to the markets thronged with people, enter the houses, pass out into the country—God fills all these places, as we have said; and yet, if you observe how all the persons you meet with are employed, you will see them thinking, talking, deliberating, busied about eatables, corn, furniture, clothes, horses, news of what is passing in the world—trifles; but who thinks of God, who sees Him, or converses about Him? And yet is it not this Ever-Present God who worketh all things? It is He that gives me light in the sun, rather than the sun itself; it is He that warms me in the fire, that refreshes me in the air I breathe, that feeds me in the nourishment I take.

The world, for the most part, spends thought enough on creatures, which the Creator, out of His bountiful goodness, makes use of for our benefit, and, for the most part, gives not a thought to the First Great Cause, which is God. Has an eminent painter produced a beautiful picture, no one stops to praise the pencil or the colours he employed: it is the painter that is thought of and that receives all the praise. O my God, Thou only art forgotten! and is it possible that our darkness is so gross? I am, I hear, I see, I love, think, taste, touch, move, not only before God, but even in Him, for by His substance He is in all parts of my body, in my veins, arteries, nerves. I rise, I lie down in God; I go and come, I walk, sit, speak, eat in the Divine Essence, and this everywhere indifferently: always, every day, all my life long, not a single moment excepted. But alas! is it not true that in almost every place, at almost every instant, we live and act and remain out of God's presence? We meet a friend, we salute him, speak to him; if we meet him somewhere else at some other time we do the same: we meet God everywhere, and everywhere we say not a word to Him, but pass Him by. The king appears in one of the public streets, and immediately all the people assume a respectful attitude; every one says, " Here is the king !" there is a rush to see him: he shows himself in another, and the same honours are paid him. O ye men, who know that God is everywhere, what respect do you pay to this Ever-Present God? Your tongue, which moves but in God, how can it utter such idle and even wicked words? How can you occupy yourselves with thoughts, designs, actions, which would make you die of shame if your poor fellow-creatures saw them? and yet you think of such things, and do them, in God! Is not this the abomination of desolation? To offend God even in God! O impure wretch, why ponder you not this truth! Were a great prince to honour you with a visit, would you not first cleanse your house, and then do your best to dress and adorn it? Remember that all the Three Divine Persons make their continual abode within you—in your heart, in the inmost centre of your soul: what pains do you take to receive Them worthily? " God is everywhere," exclaims the seraphic Teresa; "everywhere, therefore, I will endeavour to enjoy the honour of speaking to Him and looking upon Him. Here is a befitting and excellent subject of prayer for which there is no need of books, or sciences, or great systems. And further," continues the saint, "I will take great care to harbour nothing in my soul which can be displeasing in His eyes." This is how saints speak and act : what do we say and do? O appalling blindness! O frightful insensibility!

Nay, it must be confessed that, even when we do think of God, and speak of Him, and occupy ourselves about Him, and pray to Him, alas! alas! it is with a faith so weak, with aim so low, that we may be said to know Him without knowing Him. Ah! if men knew, yea but a little, what God is, with what awe would they engage in prayer, or hear His divine word, or deport themselves in His temples. Certainly, when we consider how the generality of men behave in our churches, how they speak of God—sometimes even persons who make profession of devotion—how they behave during prayer, and the little fear they have of sinning, we cannot but say there is need to go into the midst even of Christians and Catholics, and cry aloud, " To the Unknown God," proclaiming Him whom they profess to adore, but know not. Most true it is that, did we possess but a little of the true light of God, at the least mention of Him, wheresoever it might be, the soul would instantly enter into a state of holy recollection and humble itself profoundly in His Divine Presence. Miserable, wretched creatures that we are, who feel so little awe for Infinite Majesty! We speak of Him with levity, we think of Him with less attention than we bestow on the fleeting, perishable things of this life. "Woe to me," exclaimed St. Augustine, "for daring to speak to Thee, O my God." The Angelas, the Catherines accused themselves of speaking unworthily of Him, when they had been giving utterance to admirable, yea, most wonderful mysteries concerning Him.

Whoever, then, reflects on the little light we possess respecting the Deity in this wretched world, must understand at once that Jesus is hidden as He is God; but it is not easy to perceive that He is hidden also as He is man. This it is that is displayed so wonderfully in this Adorable Saviour. He is hidden at the first moment of His divinely human life in the womb of a virgin, where He abides nine full months. He is hidden in His birth in a poor stable. From His birth to the age of twelve years, and from the age of twelve years to that of thirty, He is hidden. What a history of all those years of a life so divine, every moment of which is so precious! All that we learn about it is that He was "subject" to the Most Holy Virgin and St. Joseph (Luke ii. 51)—a few words, which conceal the glories of this God-Man in such a way as must form matter of astonishment for all eternity. We know not what He said, or what He did, His occupations or His conversation, during the course of so many years. We shall show that He was hidden even when He was most visible. He was hidden in His death so utterly that He declares of Himself that He seemed as "a worm, and no man" (Psalm xxi. 7). He was hidden in the tomb after His death. But He is still more marvellously hidden in the loving abode wherein He abides with us even to the consummation of the world—the Most Holy Sacrament of the Altar. He is hidden in His mysteries; He is hidden in His

Blessed Mother; in His Apostles; in the members of His mystical body; in the sufferings and persecutions of His Church. In fine, Jesus, the God of all greatness, is hidden in everything He is; whilst man, that worm of the earth, that lump of clay, that nonentity—nothingness itself—bends all his efforts to make a show in everything; putting himself forward by his birth, if he be of good family; by his natural qualities, if he possess any; displaying his intellect, his memory, his judgment, his facility in speech, his personal beauty, his temporal goods—beautiful houses, beautiful grounds, beautiful furniture, large revenues; his gold and silver, his pleasures, his honours, his offices and employments, his credit and power, the successful issue of his affairs; and, what is most lamentable, making use sometimes of spiritual things in order to gain himself repute : as preaching, the confessional, direction, good books, good works, charitable labours, Apostolical functions, offices in the Church ; thus exalting self by all sorts of means, in every kind of way, natural and supernatural; this wretched nonentity being always desirous of exhibiting himself, while Jesus, who is All in all, remains hidden.

CHAPTER II.

JESUS HIDDEN AS TO HIS GENERATION, ETERNAL AND TEMPORAL.

No, my Lord and my God, the heaven is not so far removed from the earth as Thy ways from those of men. Thy ways are not as our ways. Man thinks as man, and Thou thinkest as God. O Uncreated Son, O Eternal Word, Thou art pleased to be born in time, and to become man, for ends infinitely glorious to Thy Father and infinitely advantageous to mankind. Thou descendest, then, upon our earth with admirable designs, and to accomplish them Thou willest to teach mankind and to save them. Certain it is that man, thinking as man, never could have devised means better calculated to ensure the success of designs so great than a distinguished birth and a brilliant life, which might attract the eyes of all the world. For does it not seem that, if Thou hadst chosen some great queen for Thy mother, and hadst appeared here below as a mighty sovereign, with all the pomp and circumstance of kingly majesty, Thou wouldst have found it far more easy to get Thy doctrine received and established, Thy maxims honoured, and Thy laws observed? Is not this what is thought and what is said every day, and even amongst Christians, who profess to take Thee as their model ?   The imagination never fails to be struck with birth, and rank, and state. Men think to work wonders in ecclesiastical offices by the splendour of a noble extraction and the display of equipages, retinue, and sumptuous living. It is seldom that in the exercise even of things the most divine we cease from what is human.   We look at the supernatural with the eyes of the flesh, and measure the ways of grace by the policy of human prudence. The numerous examples of persons eminent in sanctity, which every century of the New Law presents to us, make scarcely any impression on our minds. The long experience of so many hundred years does not dispel the darkness that surrounds us, although it shows us most clearly that, as well for the execution of His greatest designs as for the publication of the Gospel in lands where it had not hitherto been preached, God has made use of the very same means which He adopted when He became man; choosing for himself the poor and abject of this world, or such as concealed their noble birth, if noble it chanced to be, in the obscurity of an ignoble life, and made themselves poor if they were rich.   The Spirit of God is ever the Spirit of God, and the spirit of man remains ever the spirit of man, unless, by going out of itself, it allows itself to be raised by the help of grace to that which is supernatural and divine ; and this can be effected only by a diligent and faithful practice of that self-renunciation which Jesus Christ requires of all His disciples.

O men, I invite you to draw nigh in spirit to the birth-place of your God, and you especially who pride yourselves on your noble origin. Ecclesiastics, who think to base your influence on the vain distinction of an illustrious birth, behold this Infant in the crib, whom you acknowledge as your God; and tell me, is this, then, that Divine Word, the image of the Eternal Father, the brightness of His glory and the figure of His substance, begotten from all eternity in His bosom? What! He who hath no beginning, does He vouchsafe to be born in time? He whom the heaven and the earth cannot contain, does He shut Himself up in the womb of a young virgin? He who is infinite, does He limit Himself to the form of a little child? Contemplate awhile this Divine Infant, and you will see that He hides in an ineffable manner all the splendours of His eternal generation; yea, He hides them so effectually that the great Apostle declares, by the inspiration of the Holy Ghost, that He *annihilated* Himself.*

Let us consider also that this dear Infant, who, as man, is descended from the blood of so many kings, conceals all His glory by choosing to be born of the wife of a poor carpenter. He, who is innocence itself, wills, in the order of His Providence, that in His temporal genealogy should be enumerated women who were sinners, to teach us to make light of family nobility; not to value ourselves upon it, or bring it into notice; not to be ashamed of our relatives if they are poor or humble, or have fallen into disgrace. The saints, who were filled with the Spirit of our Lord, neglected nothing by which they might hide their noble birth : they even had recourse to holy stratagems to prevent their being known as persons of rank, and suffered much when they were esteemed for their

* Phil. ii. 7: the Greek text signifies " He emptied Himself," or " made Himself void "—reduced Himself, as it were, to nothingness.

high connections. But they who are influenced by a spirit merely human, are ready enough to speak, or, at least, are not sorry when others speak, of their extraction, and are ingenious in furnishing occasions for its mention, or, if they are not persons of family, they try their utmost to conceal it, anxiously avoid every occasion which might betray their origin, and are annoyed when they cannot prevent such disclosure; and, what is most astonishing, this weakness is to be met with even in many ecclesiastics and religious, nay, even in preachers, confessors, and directors. Where is there to be found one who desires to be buried with Jesus in the tomb of a hidden life? Alas! what shall we say of those Christians who take such pride in their birth, and make their worldly rank the occasion of so much quarrelling and of so many evils? Yet they call themselves Christians, the disciples of a God-Man, who was pleased to pass for the son of a carpenter; who did not think it derogatory to His priestly or episcopal office, or a hindrance to the blessed effects of His mission, or in any way a restriction on its operations, to expose Himself to the reproaches cast upon Him for the meanness of His birth: as is related by St. Matthew (xiii. 55), who writes that the people of Nazareth, when they heard Him preach, said, "Is not this the carpenter's son?" and St. Mark declares (vi. 3), that they said, "Is not this the carpenter, the son of Mary?"

CHAPTER III.

JESUS HIDDEN AS TO HIS NATURAL QUALITIES.

IT is an undoubted truth that the Adorable Jesus possessed the most capacious and the most powerful mind that ever was, the most felicitous memory, the most solid judgment, the most exquisite imagination, and every sense, interior and exterior, in the most perfect harmony ; but it is no less indubitable, on the other hand, that He concealed all these natural gifts in a most wonderful manner. What divine and marvellous books might He have composed, had He been pleased to write ! Would He not have produced truly heavenly works ? His thoughts, His reasonings, His illuminations—would they not have been enough to transport with admiration and love every intelligence in heaven and in earth ? Would not His writings have abounded in the richest and most precious stores of all imaginable sciences ? O my adorable Master, as I meditate on this truth I am overwhelmed with shame and confusion. What am I that I should indeed dare to write of Thy divine mysteries ? And yet it would seem as if such were Thy will, and that the requests of Thy servants of both sexes were Thine own command. O my Lord and my God, I entreat Thy pardon for my boldness in venturing to speak and write of Thee. Forgive, O my amiable Saviour, a wretched sinner, a foul and putrid dog, who deserves only Thy eternal anger and the torments of the damned. I pray and beseech my brethren and sisters in Christ, who shall read my little works, to intercede for me with Thy Divine Majesty, that I may obtain pardon and grace. O blessed angels, and thou in particular, O immortal spirit, who art appointed to be my guardian; O all ye holy men and women, saints of God, be you my advocates before His Infinite Majesty, that He may not cast me away from His Divine Presence. And can it be that I may venture to speak of my God—I who am nothing but dust and ashes? Our age has beheld a man full of grace and light, gifted with an angelic spirit, the late Father de Condren, who, when he was urged to write, made this truly Christian answer: "Who could have written more worthily and more holily than Jesus our Divine Master? and yet He did not. How, then, can you wish that I should write?" This truth must for ever prevent our writing for distinction's sake, or of our own natural impulse, or for any other motive than the cause of God alone; and more than this, we must have a call from grace and a suggestion from the Holy Spirit. This is why we must never be precipitate, and must undertake nothing save with fear and trembling. Moreover, we ought to have a horror, and an extreme horror, lest self-love should mingle anything of its own with works composed even in compliance with a movement of grace, as the affectation of fine language, curious speculations, and such-like things, remembering that the kingdom of God is not set up in the eloquence of man, but in the power of God. He was pleased that His divine word should be committed to writing by those who were mean and little in the world's eyes, in a simple, unaffected style, to confound man's wisdom and overthrow the policy of the prudent of this world.

But besides all this, Jesus, that Divine Master sent to us by the Eternal Father, who even caused His voice to be heard from heaven, to teach us that it was His will that we should hearken to Him, instructed the souls of men in a plain familiar way, and made use of similitudes, as unlearned persons are wont to do; He taught a doctrine which drew down upon Him the derision and scorn of many, as is related in the Gospel, and especially of the rich and covetous, who made a mock of His discourses. O ye Christians, who pride yourselves on your intellectual powers, come and behold your God before an earthly king : see how He is content to pass for a fool; how He is treated as one who has lost his reason ; and is made the laughing-stock of a whole court. Come and behold Him seized, not by His enemies or strangers, but by His relatives, who take Him for a madman. Learn hence the value you ought to set on the reputation attached to literature, science, and intellectual superiority. Ye men of learning, humble yourselves at a sight so astounding as that of a God-Man accounted, not only to possess no surpassing intellect, but to have altogether lost His mind. Surely, surely, did we believe what we profess to believe, could we possibly wish to be thought highly of by the world ? O ye Christian ladies, who, out of vanity and self-love, delight in possessing and reading difficult books, books that discuss the abstrusest questions of the schools—for instance, such as treat of grace; who pride yourselves on elegance of language and a ready wit; turn your eyes on Jesus, your God, and then, if one spark of faith remains to you, sink into an abyss of confusion at His feet. Jesus is God, and Jesus the God desires to destroy the vanity of man; He is pleased to pass for a madman before the highest persons in the world, even a king and all his court: and a worm of the earth, who calls himself His disciple, would wish to be admired for his intellect and knowledge; surely this is intolerable presumption. Ye men of genius, remember the little account that God makes of mental powers, seeing that He has left them in perpetual possession to the devils, His declared enemies. Be comforted, ye poor and simple men and women, in your littleness, so only that it be accompanied with humility, for this it is on which God sets a value: and of this the devils will never be able to perform the slightest act.

Moreover, we must add that Jesus, the fairest among the children of men, hid the beauty of His Divine countenance amidst the dust of a mean workshop, where He remained secluded nearly all His life, and at last concealed all its comeliness under the spittings wherewith it was covered in the time of His dolorous Passion, when He appeared so disfigured that He became as a leper, as Scripture says. O blessed they who, in imitation of this Divine model, set little store by personal beauty! O blessed those religious houses which conceal it from the world's sight behind close-curtained grates! Such souls will appear with confidence, at the moment of death, before the eyes of a Judge to whom alone they have endeavoured to render themselves pleasing. But a terrible judgment is reserved for those who have set such value on the beauty of their persons, and have spent so much delicate care upon it, and taken so much vain complacency in it; who have sought their pleasure in seeing creatures and being seen by them, and thus have engrossed minds and hearts formed for God alone, robbing and defrauding Him of them with a shamelessness truly shocking. Oh, what terror will seize on these unhappy souls, when they shall come before the tremendous judgment-seat of God! Then let them call upon those whom they have sought to please, that they may come to their assistance on this their day of account: then will be seen the illusion and the vanity of personal beauty. But alas! there will no longer be time to undo those attachments to creatures which this beauty has occasioned. Woe to us, if the love and reverent thought of God cannot set us free from vanities which the inevitable necessity of death will force us to quit! O ye who read this, pause awhile to think upon these truths; ponder them deliberately and with much serious reflection.

In fine, Jesus, whose lovely disposition, sweetness of demeanour, and engaging discourse were all full of divine attractions, perceiving that His disciples were becoming attached to these things, albeit so innocent, declared to them that it was expedient that He should leave them, seeing that they hindered the coming of the Holy Spirit, whom He desired to send them; and thus retiring from their sight, He deprived them of His bodily presence, and at the same time withdrew from them all the charms of His conversation in the flesh. Let us linger here awhile to consider more deeply this conduct of a Man-God. Yes, it is a Man-God who conceals the natural attractions of His Sacred Humanity, lest men, in their imperfection, should become attached to them; and we, wretched creatures as we are, so far from hiding whatever little natural perfections we may possess, seek occasions, or readily profit by such as may present themselves, to make a display of our cleverness, our wit, or our agreeable powers of conversation ; or to show that we are not devoid of literary knowledge, that we possess a certain learning, and are experienced in affairs ; that we can speak well, write well, sing well, and so forth. But more than this, and I must call it a disorder which we ought to lament with tears of blood, it is but too true that the self-love of the creature is so preposterous and so extravagant that it even goes the length of wishing to be preferred before God Himself. This is only too apparent in those who study to be seen or heard in churches and places wholly consecrated to God.   Yes, this man or this woman of the world wishes to be the object of observation in our very churches, actually disputing in sacrilegious impiety precedence with the Sovereign Majesty who resides therein in so adorable a manner.   These fine voices want to be listened to and to engage affections due to the Lord of all, whose very worship must subserve their purposes, with a perversion the most monstrous that it is possible to conceive. Ecclesiastics, beware of carrying this disorder into the very sanctuary, and even to the altar.   Religious, beware of admitting it into your cloisters and your churches. Learn that God alone merits to engross all minds and hearts ; that we ought never to say anything or do anything except for His honour and love.   Alas ! for ourselves, we deserve only confusion and disgrace.

I conclude this chapter with what is related of that holy man, Father de Condren, who, having naturally a very sweet and musical voice, did his best to speak a little through his nose, for fear of pleasing, and that he might not arrest the attention of his hearers by the agreeableness of his delivery. Thus did he desire but God only, to whom he was continually sacrificing all things.

CHAPTER IV.

JESUS HIDDEN IN HIS PRIVATION OF TEMPORAL GOODS.

As it is the happiness of earthly sovereigns to possess much temporal goods and enjoy large revenues, it would seem that to be a king and to be rich were one and the same; and, in truth, it would be most difficult to persuade ourselves, whatever might be told us, on meeting a poor man, that he was a monarch, the sovereign of some flourishing kingdom. It is the prerogative of Jesus to be the King of kings, the Lord of lords, and at the same time the poorest man on earth. Oh, who ever heard of poverty so extreme in a royal personage? At His birth His palace was a wretched stable; His courtiers were brute animals; instead of tapestry and furniture He had but bare walls and spiders' webs; His cradle was a manger, with a little straw and hay; His only protection in the midst of a cold night, an open stable, exposed to the inclemency of the weather and to all the discomforts of the wintry season. As time goes on, He will eat His bread in the sweat of his brow, maintaining Himself by the labour of His hands, exercising the trade of a carpenter; or He will live on alms, the offering of holy women who follow Him in His journeys, as is related in the Gospel (Luke viii. 3). In fine, at the hour of death He will be stripped of everything, not even possessing a piece of linen to cover His nakedness when exposed upon the Cross. And whilst the birds of the air have their nests and the foxes their holes, the Son of Man will have nowhere to lay His head (Matt. viii. 20).

O amiable Jesus, in very truth the strong and loving affections of Thy heart lead Thee to hide Thyself in every way. O men, what signs of royalty can you discover, with all the lights that nature affords you, in the midst of a poverty so fearful and repulsive? O my soul, is He whom thou beholdest all naked on a gibbet, the Lord to whom belong the world and the whole compass of the earth? O my Lord, it is faith alone that reveals to me amid such utter spoliation, that Thou art the King of Ages, the King of Angels and of Men, the Absolute Master of the whole universe. It is this sight which faith unveils, that has touched so powerfully the hearts of many kings and queens, and of many princes and princesses, who, voluntarily quitting their kingdoms and principalities, preferred the obscurity of a solitude and a cloister to all the glory and dignity of their earthly crown. This sight it is that has led so many rich persons to despoil themselves of their goods, and bury themselves alive in the tomb of religion. Oh, how much better to live unknown and despised in the house of the Lord than to dwell with pomp and applause in the palaces of the great ones of this world!

And yet it must be confessed that voluntary poverty, so praiseworthy as being the free choice of a state recommended by the mouth of God Himself, and which, on this account, and by the practice of holy vows, possesses so many advantages above compulsory poverty, does not commonly involve the loss of the esteem and praise of men. It carries with it a greater honour than it renounces, and, in flying from glory, it finds it more abundantly. This is not the case with compulsory poverty, the practice of which involves no danger, since, without all doubt, it is in the order of the will of God, for its very necessity hides all that is most exalted, most Christian, and most holy in its exercise. As it is contemptible in the eyes of men, it shelters those who suffer it from their esteem, and thus admits them to a deeper participation in the poor and abject life of the Son of God. This truth is most consoling for such as are poor by birth, or reduced to poverty by change of circumstances, or other vicissitudes.

But the pride, the arrogance, and the vanity of the creature cannot endure the degradation which the state of poverty entails. They who are born in poverty complain and deem themselves unfortunate, not perceiving the honour that God does them, in giving them a life so closely allied to that which He chose for the love of us. Others give way to impatience, and murmur; and it is difficult to persuade them to allow their minds any rest, remaining immersed as they do in mere nature, without raising themselves by the help of divine grace to those views which faith unfolds to us of a state so conducive to the salvation of souls, and one that yields so much glory to God. Strange phenomenon, this pride of the creature in its corruption! You will see people of low origin, and destitute of all earthly and temporal goods, and labouring at mean and sordid trades, who are anxious not to be regarded as altogether paupers. If they are in want, they will be ashamed of being relieved, unless it be in secret; they cannot get themselves without a struggle to make their distress known, when in no other way can they be assisted. Whatever be a man's condition, he will conceal his poverty, such shame does all the world feel for the livery of Jesus Christ. I will say more: you will see people who profess particular devotion, who esteem and love poverty, who even rejoice in their necessities, who are careful not to possess anything superfluous, who are even ready to dispense with many of the necessaries of life, if their director so enjoins, but all this on condition of being exempted from the contempt of poverty. Such persons will suffer as much poverty as you please, provided it is not known; or, if it be so, provided it is supposed to be voluntary, embraced from a Christian motive and out of virtue, and not from necessity. Separate from it whatever is held in repute, or, rather, join thereto the contempt and disgrace which this state, when it is compulsory, commonly carries with it, and these devout men and women will feel themselves humiliated, if their necessities are known; they must be humoured, like other people, on this point of honour; they will dissemble and equivocate to conceal their state, and they will take care to have nothing and to do nothing which can make it known. O Adorable Jesus, how few are there who are willing to hide themselves with Thee from the eyes of men, by a life of poverty, a life abject and despised!

CHAPTER V.

Jesus Hidden in His Privation of the Esteem and Friendship of Creatures.

St. Augustine remarks that there is one temptation which attaches itself so closely to our corrupt nature, that he doubts whether it ceases during the whole course of this mortal life. This temptation consists in the desire we feel of sharing the esteem and friendship of creatures. It is most evident that the generality of men are not only assailed by this very temptation, but that they yield to it and give themselves up to it without a struggle. The creature is engrossed with the creature and utterly estranged from the Creator. Oh! how rare it is to find souls to whom God alone suffices. Few say in sincerity those words of St. Francis of Assisi, so humble of heart and so separated from the world :—" My God and my all; my God and my all." When we have shaken off all attachment to persons of the world, we betake ourselves, and sometimes insensibly, to those who belong to God. Nor do we fail to have some specious pretext. We say, such a one is a holy man, or a holy woman—a superior or superioress—a director—a confessor ; and indeed we ought to have consideration and respect for such persons. Nor, under pretext of disengagement, must we neglect the aids which God bestows upon us by their means ; but at the same time we must take care that our regard for them be free from all attachment and eager desire for their esteem and friendship ; for, in few words, Christian self-renunciation can brook no reserve.   We must die to all creatures whatsoever, to all trust in them and reliance upon them, and all desire of their approbation, and must dispose ourselves to be deprived of them when it shall please Divine Providence so to ordain.   A holy soul, the Venerable Mother Magdalen of St. Joseph, a Carmelite nun, and prioress of the Convent of the Incarnation, in the Faubourg St. Jacques, a soul of extraordinary mortification, eminent virtue, admirable piety, and heavenly conversation, and one greatly honoured by our Lord and the glorious Virgin, both before and after her precious death —this holy soul, I say, maintained that even good people ought to be banished from our heart as well as others. Alas ! it is very sad to see how persons, even such as are devout, allow their minds to be amused by creatures, and how nature predominates in the discourses and conversations which they hold together ; in the very midst of their spiritual exercises, their good works, charitable labours, and their very holiest undertakings.   O my God, what subtle self-seekings, what secret complacencies in their intercourse with each other, and in the pleasure that is felt in such intimacies, though in themselves good !   How completely taken by surprise would most of these persons be if they were no longer made any use of, if they were repulsed, and even blamed by the devout ; for as for the ill-opinion of others they do not distress themselves so much about it.   The reason of all this is that we are always desiring to have a share, and that sometimes unconsciously, in the esteem and friendship of creatures. As many good works as you will, labours and superabundant labours, for our neighbour's good ; extraordinary penances, large alms-deeds, great and toilsome undertakings, preaching, hearing confessions, going on missions, all these are to be met with, and praise be to our Lord and His most holy Mother for it, for they are means of glorifying our Divine King and Lord of all ; but where will you find a spirit poor and stripped of all things—a heart as entirely empty of every created thing, as if there were but God alone and itself in the whole world,— free from human aims and all regard to creatures, placing its joy in being forsaken by them, deprived of them, cast out by them, and despised, troubling itself no more about them than if they did not exist ?

Such nevertheless is the example which Jesus has given us. Oh, how much it is to be wished that this divine model were more copied by Christians ! But what are you doing, O ye who profess an especial devotion towards Him, if you neglect to regulate your life and actions by this pattern which the Eternal Father has given you ? What will be your astonishment when you die ! And he who passed for a person of extraordinary devotion, because he practised great austerities, or employed himself in works of mercy—of what little account will he be in the sight of God his judge, who stops not at appearances and outside show, but looks at the heart and at the soul denuded of all things ?

O my soul, let us direct all our attention to the dear Jesus, who suffers an utter privation of all creatures, that He may teach us in what contempt we ought to hold them; and that it is God alone on whom we ought to fix our regard. Jesus is so little esteemed among men, that at the end we shall see a whole populace demand His death, and cry with a loud voice, "Crucify Him." The authorities of the place and the governor condemn Him. A king treats Him as a fool. The doctors of the law and the priests draw up His accusation. The high priest declares Him worthy of death. His own disciples take to flight and desert Him; and the most zealous amongst them does not dare to confess before a poor maid-servant that he knows Him: he denies Him even with an oath. O my good Saviour, what share hadst Thou then in the minds and hearts of creatures? But, O my soul, shall we not associate ourselves with this God-Man in His great, His extreme privations! And after such a sight, can we retain any desire for the esteem or friendship of the creatures of this vile world?

CHAPTER VI.

JESUS HIDDEN IN IGNOMINIES.

THERE are very different ways of leading a hidden life. Some hide themselves by retiring into solitudes and living in deserts; others by leading an ordinary life, and avoiding all singularity. But it must be confessed that nothing hides us more than contempt and ignominy. They who live in solitudes, though banished from the eyes of men, often retain a place in their mind and heart, through the admiration excited by their detachment from the world, and the peculiar esteem with which virtue is still regarded by mankind. Thus you will find solitaries making a great noise in the world : people are eager to go and see them ; they are talked about, and form the subject of conversation in large companies ; and they may be said to be never more known than when they are most retired and least known. They who lead an ordinary life in the world, whatever pains they may take to escape observation, will hardly, after all, prevent men from recognizing their virtue, and bestowing upon them the approbation it so justly deserves. It is to contempt and ignominy that is reserved the privilege of a life entirely hidden. One whose life is spoken against, whose goodness passes for hypocrisy, whose innocence is covered with calumny, is more hidden than if he lived in deserts, seeing that he is annihilated in the minds and hearts of men by the disdain and contempt with which they regard him. O Christian, whoever thou art, wheresoever thy abode, rejoice and bless God, and render Him a thousand thanks, together with His most holy Mother, if thou be traduced and deprived of thy good name. It is the sure and excellent way of entering into the unknown life of thy God and Saviour. Wherefore art thou sad, and why dost thou grieve, at seeing thyself the contempt and scorn of men ? Ah ! if thou didst but know the gift of God ; if thou didst but discern the tenderness of Divine Providence towards thy soul ! Oh, how holy and how profitable to be cast out of the mind and heart of creatures—to be united and to become truly one with the mind and heart of Jesus. It is good, then, that the Lord should humble us, that we should

be hated by good men and bad, by strangers and relatives, by our adversaries and our friends, and by all
creatures whatsoever. O great and solid truth! Would
to God that it were better known, not only among
people of the world, but also in the cloister! Where
there is least of creatures there is most of God. O
God only, God only, God only!

This great truth it is that the Adorable Jesus
preaches to us so irresistibly by the all-powerful example of His divine life, a life covered with shame
and ignominy. Certainly, as we thus regard Him,
we may well say, "Verily, Thou art a Hidden God."
(Isaias xlv. 15.) Here words and thoughts alike fail
us; the very spirit within us faints away, and we are
lost in an abyss of amazement, whence there is no
arising. O Infinite Greatness! O Creator of the
universe! O Sovereign King of angels and of men!
and is it Thou before whom robbers and murderers
are preferred? O Wisdom Increate, O Well-Beloved
Son of the Eternal Father, is it, then, Thou who art
counted a fool and a madman in the court of the
kings of the earth? Is it Thou, O my God, who
passest for an impostor, a malefactor, one possessed
by a devil, and a hypocrite? Hearken, O ye men;
hearken, O ye angels of heaven. Is it a God who is
condemned to death, who is fastened to a gibbet? O
spectacle strange and unheard-of! "Verily"—let us
repeat it again—it is in these ignominies, O Adorable
Jesus, that "Thou art a Hidden God." Truths so
vast and astounding, told in so few words, merit the
attention of our whole life and of a long and endless
eternity. O worm of the earth, who art ever anxious
to exhibit thyself; wretched nonentity, unhappy
sinner, who art ever wishing to make a show in the

world, canst thou help dying of very shame at the sight of the self-annihilations of thy God? After beholding all this, canst thou still retain any desire of being known and esteemed? Ah! my Sovereign Lord, Thou art treated like one who has lost his mind, and shall I pride myself on my mental powers? Men desire to be thought wise, learned, and experienced in affairs. Thou placest Thyself below the feet of the very vilest, and we long for nothing but to be exalted. We lay stress on a point of honour, whilst Thou art robbed of Thy reputation. And shall we, then, complain of any treatment we may receive, however grievous and unjust it may appear to us? Ah! my Lord, my Divine King, is it that we are more innocent than Thou, or more worthy of consideration? Is it that our sufferings exceed Thine, or that our humiliations are greater than Thy abasement? Let us go, O my soul, let us go, at whatever cost of health, life, reputation, friends—let us go up on Calvary with our Adorable King; let us bear Him company, together with His most holy Mother and the beloved disciple. Let us go and die with Him: let us die to points of honour, attachment to temporal goods, the pleasures of the body; let us die to creatures, to our friends and relatives; let us die to everything, that, living no longer to ourselves, or for ourselves, we may live henceforth only the life of Jesus—a life separate from the world, a life hidden in God, and in God only. O God only, God only, God only! O my soul, my soul, far better is it to be afflicted, dishonoured, poor, abandoned here below with Jesus, and thus to enter into His hidden life in God, that we may be glorified and manifested with this dear Saviour for all eternity, than to enjoy the pleasures and the honours of the world in this present life, in the company of worldlings, to make a stir and show among men, and then go down to the darkness of hell, there to suffer the horrible confusion of the damned for ever. O ye who read this, I conjure you firmly to resolve to reflect upon these truths with close attention; and to make them from time to time the subject of your meditations for the remainder of your days.

CHAPTER VII.

Jesus Hidden as to His Power.

IF you closely observe the ordinary conduct of Christians, you will see that it is wholly opposed to that of Jesus. It is strange that men, who are made to the image of God, should efface almost every feature of resemblance by their sins: but what is altogether astounding is to see Christians, who profess to be followers of Jesus Christ, walking in ways altogether divergent from His. They believe in all His words as undeniable truths, and hold them to be oracles so sure, so holy, so divine, that they protest they are ready to give their life to maintain them; and yet, to see them act, it would appear as if they believed nothing of all they profess to believe, and that the Gospel was for them a fable. They belie their words by their actions; and while making profession of Christianity, which necessarily implies the imitation of Jesus Christ, they lead the life of infidels; and, what is most deplorable, their life is sometimes even worse than that of infidels, so attached are they to this corrupt world, and so estranged in their inclinations from Jesus, the divine model which ought to serve them as their rule. This truth needs no other proof than that of universal experience, which leaves us no room for doubt. It is sensibly displayed in most of the actions of Christians, in which it would be very difficult to discern the relation they ought to have to the actions of the Son of God, particularly as respects His ¦hidden life and the strong love He manifested for a life so retired and so holy. Woe to us, who do the very contrary of what we ought to do! In truth we are only poor miserable nothings, and we are always desiring to be something. Jesus is All in all, and in all things Jesus annihilates Himself.

But how entire is this His self-annihilation! All power was given Him, as He Himself said, in heaven and in earth, and He hides all His divine powers under the appearance of exceeding weakness. What weakness greater than that of a child? If we regarded these things merely humanly, who could ever have had the least conception that the hands of a babe wrapped in swaddling-clothes, themselves enveloped in swathing-bands, were the hands of Him who fashioned the whole world; that a speechless child was the Very Word Himself, the Eternal Word of an Eternal Father; that an infant who makes known his wants only by childish cries and tears, was He whose voice makes itself heard even by that which is not; who commands the winds and the tempests; whom all created things obey? Who could suppose that He who bears in His hands all the mighty fabric of the universe, should be dependent upon a young virgin, to be carried in her arms whithersoever He goes; that He who supplies both man and beast with food, should be nourished with a little milk received from a creature? Can He more completely hide His Omnipotence than by fleeing before a mortal man, as though He stood in fear of him? And the dread of death, to which He abandoned Himself in the Garden of Olives, was it not a sign of great weakness? So great was it, that it made Him shed such an amazing quantity of blood that it flowed in streams down to the ground. Certainly it must be said that this amiable God-Man displayed an extraordinary desire to conceal His powers. He appears before Herod, He appears before Pilate, both of whom had heard of the miracles He wrought, and desired greatly to see some performed by Him: and does it not seem, judging by appearances, that it was fitting to satisfy them for the glory of His Father, and for the glory of what He Himself was? And yet this Divine Saviour would work no miracle before this king or this governor, though the refusal was to cost Him His reputation and His life; thus preferring the hidden life to His honour, and even to life itself; paying no heed to all the specious pretexts that might have been urged upon Him. It is in the same incomparable manner that He acts upon the cross. They call upon Him to show His power by coming down from the cross, and they would believe in Him; but, whatever men may say, and whatever they may do, nothing can separate Him from the love of the hidden life.

We said at the commencement of this chapter that our conduct was generally quite opposed to that of Jesus Christ, and the truth of this remark is particularly apparent in the subject of which we are treating. From the moment sin came into the world weakness has been our heritage, and we neglect nothing which may serve either to keep out of sight what we are, or to make us seem what we are not. If we enter into ourselves, we shall become conscious of the most pitiable weaknesses, of nothing but lapses and relapses, blindness, sin upon sin. We allow ourselves to be overcome by the merest nothings; an inclination, a pleasure, a phantom of honour, a trifle, an offensive word are enough to overpower and conquer us. We have no strength in ourselves, as of ourselves, to resist the least temptations, as Christians ought; and yet we wish to pass for persons who are able to command their passions, and should feel greatly ashamed at having our weaknesses known. We wish to seem endowed with strength in natural things—strength of mind, memory, judgment—with discretion in our affairs, our resolutions and counsels, in our words and reasonings, in our writings and undertakings. We wish to seem of importance by our wealth and possessions, our station and office, our resources and connections, our friends, and the interest we possess with influential persons. Our manner of proceeding is the same in supernatural things; we wish to appear mighty in works and in words, in the great results they produce, in the large number of persons of consequence who highly esteem our teaching or our direction, and in the striking actions we perform in public; the amount of our alms, our severe austerities, the sublime knowledge we possess of the spiritual life, and extraordinary graces. Man, Christian man, can with difficulty keep from displaying whatever talents he possesses; he wishes to be thought powerful, nor does he want for pretexts which have a show even of consulting the glory of God. We conclude, then, that we ought to set before us Jesus Christ and His divine example as the sacred model on which all our actions should be framed.

CHAPTER VIII.

Jesus Hidden as to His Offices and Dignities.

The Holy Spirit teaches us in the Divine Epistles that Jesus Christ did not of Himself assume the Pontificate, but being ordained thereto by His Father, was made the Shepherd and Bishop of Souls. It is, then, an undeniable truth that the Adorable Jesus was a bishop; nor can we doubt this truth without sin, seeing that it is contained in the Sacred Books. He exercised His office with a charity so excessive, and with a solicitude so tender and so strong, as to cost Him His life, dying on Calvary for all mankind, like a good pastor for his flock. But it must be acknowledged that He was invested with this high dignity, and that He discharged all its functions and bore all its burdens, without accepting any of the honour and glory which usually accompany it.

Jesus is destined by His Father for the Episcopate; He comes into the world as the Bishop of Souls. But it will be a bishop all poor and abject, leading a life of sorrow and contempt, one who will appear in the world as a worm of the earth, and the scorn of men. O Holy and Adorable Pontiff, what signs dost

Thou show of the greatness of Thy Pontificate? Where is its splendour and its glory? Instead of revenues and riches, I behold Thee suffering a most rigorous and extreme poverty. Thou hast a stable for Thy palace, and instead of country-houses, a borrowed lodging, and many times the bare earth alone to rest upon at night, finding nowhere a roof to cover Thee, as Thou didst reveal to the seraphic Saint Teresa. For equipage Thou hast a mean animal, an ass; Thy whole retinue is not merely limited to one or two servants, some scanty number of attendants, but, O wonderful thought! Thou hast not one to wait upon Thee. And even so Thou didst sweetly say (Matt. xx. 28) that Thou wast come, not to be ministered unto, but to minister. If Thou establishest an Apostolical college, it will be composed of illiterate persons—fishermen, such as shall move the world to scorn and derision. Thine altar shall be a cross, which shall be stained with Thine own Blood; and Thyself shall be the victim immolated thereon in the midst of Thy people. O Good Shepherd, Thou shalt be sacrificed by Thine own flock, who, far from hearkening to Thy pastoral voice, shall repay Thy divine teaching only with mockery and contempt. The shouts which the people raise around Thee, shall not be acclamations of joy and loud applause, but savage and insulting cries calling for Thy death. Thou shalt go alone, O Divine Pontiff, to the sacrifice, abandoned by Thy priests, rejected, mocked, hated, put to death by Thine own subjects, who shall strip Thee of Thy very garments, leaving Thee all naked, exposed to the hootings and the jeers of a whole rabble.

In such guise was it that the Eternal Father sent His Well-Beloved Son. Behold the revenues, the riches, the delights, the joys, the honours, and the grandeurs of His Episcopate! It is related of the glorious St. Martin, Bishop of Tours, that, penetrated with these thoughts, he sighed only after a poor and abject life. He wore only mean coarse garments, and neglected nothing, or, rather, used every possible endeavour, to escape the honours paid to his dignity and personal merits. For this purpose he preferred walking alone, bidding his ecclesiastics not to follow him except at a distance, because he hoped by this means not to be recognized, and consequently not only to avoid the respect usually shown him, but on the contrary, to be the object of scorn and insult on account of the poverty and meanness of his dress, to which we have alluded. And, in fact, by this mode of proceeding he succeeded in his wishes, since it gave occasion, as history relates, to his meeting not only with contempt, but with blows and cruel treatment. After all, it is most worthy of our attention that Jesus, as man, came of a royal lineage and of the blood of the greatest kings of the earth, not to say, moreover, that He was the Son of God; and yet the consideration of His birth and of His exalted character, royal and divine, did not make this Bishop of our souls abate anything of the poor and abject state which He was pleased to assume. Never was there a higher, a more glorious, or a more divine office, or one which involved greater consequences; seeing that it was question of reconciling the whole world with God, delivering all mankind from hell for ever, and securing to them Paradise, and, with Paradise, a kingdom without end; seeing that it was question of satisfying with a most rigorous justice a God, offended by the sins of His creatures. Assuredly, then, the success of such an office was of infinite importance. And nevertheless Jesus, our Divine Pontiff, discharges it only amid poverty, contempt, and suffering, although He is the Son of God and, as man, is descended from a line of kings. O my God—never can we be weary of repeating it—Thy ways are far removed from those of men, and often even from the ways of those who profess to serve Thee. Oh, how few souls are deeply penetrated with this truth, and how rare is the practice of it! Alas! it seems to us impossible to succeed without temporal support and worldly display.

I conclude by calling attention again to a most astonishing truth, of which I said something at the beginning of this chapter. Jesus did not assume the Pontificate of Himself, as Holy Scripture testifies. I know not, after this, what excuse a man can allege in defence of his desiring and seeking after offices. I do not mean those who aspire to dignities, offices, and employments with evil intentions, and who make use of unlawful means to attain them; as, for example, such as procure benefices by purchasing the yearly revenues of the incumbents, who agree to resign in their favour, for more than they are worth, or their furniture, or other things of a like kind. As these persons carry with them their own condemnation and the plain malediction of God, I say nothing of them, and still less of those who do yet worse. I confine myself to such as say they are actuated by good intentions, and, in truth, are well-meaning persons. I allude to those who are endowed with great natural talents, fitting them to serve as instruments of grace and to acquit themselves admirably in any office they may fill. I would ask them whether Jesus Christ

was not possessed of every good quality, and whether
His intentions were not perfectly holy; and yet, if
He venture not to take a self-assumed office, how
shall another dare to do so? How shall a wretched
creature so presume, be his merits what they may?
Well might we cry out on every side against the
blindness of men; well might we cry aloud through
all the earth, "Unless the Lord build the house, they
labour in 'vain that build it" (Psalm cxxvi. 1). A
divine vocation is necessary: it is not enough to have
great abilities for good; it is not enough to be
actuated by the best intentions in the world; God
must also require of us that which we desire
to do, and we must desire nothing, not even what
is good, save the good He would have us to do.
Oh, what cause have we to weep over those pro-
fessed devout persons, who destine their children,
relatives, or friends to benefices, imagining they are
serving God, because it is their intention to do so,
and because they place them in seminaries and have
them piously educated, as if seminaries could give a
vocation to those who have it not! Experience
affords proofs enough of the unhappy results of such
designs on the part of these otherwise pious people,
who wish to do good, it is true, but wish to do it in
their own way, and not according to the will of God,
which is often opposed to the thoughts and intentions
of men; God not calling to the ecclesiastical state
those whom men destine thereto, and choosing for it
those whom men wish to keep in the world. I say it
again, we ought to weep bitterly, especially when
we think of persons raised to high ecclesiastical
dignities, irreproachable in their moral conduct and
even possessed of much piety, who let themselves be

blinded in the bestowal of benefices, offices, and employments, by a secret love of flesh and blood, or some condescension to private recommendations, or some wish of recompensing individuals to whom they are under obligations. O miserable conduct, worthy of being lamented with tears of blood! In this way official situations and other employments in the ecclesiastical court will be given away, as well as posts of considerable trust in the ecclesiastical state, abbeys, priories, benefices,—nay, strange to say, persons of tender conscience, who on occasions have scruples about such proceedings, meet with those who persuade them to disregard their feelings of remorse, and are rash enough to give them such advice, and sometimes even at the very hour of death. Oh, when will it be that men shall no longer look but to God only? O my Divine King, O Adorable Jesus, when will it be that they shall have regard only to Thy interests, and no longer be solicitous about human aims and human respects, flesh and blood, and their own wretched self-interest; when they shall await Thy commands, made known to them in ways, ordinary indeed, but holy and disinterested; when they shall no longer wish to subject Thy will to that of creatures, following in simplicity Thy leadings, and not forestalling them by a choice of state, either for themselves or for others?

I have sometimes thought with great surprise and dread of those who try to procure the tonsure for young children, in order to secure to them the possession of some of the Church's goods, and who often involve them in the manifest peril of eternal damnation, either through their maladministration of this property, which is spent without due regard to the fact that what remains after necessary wants have been supplied, belongs to the poor; or because, these revenues being the source from whence their maintenance is supplied, they continue in the ecclesiastical state without leading an ecclesiastical life, with no other vocation than the motive of living more comfortably. For, indeed, what can a youth or a younger son do, to whom his family allows no other fortune for him to live upon and support his state and rank in the world, than what is derived from benefices? On the one hand, he has no vocation for the ecclesiastical state; on the other, if he leaves it, his friends give him up, and make him no allowance to maintain himself suitably to his rank. So he continues in his state, and does ill in so continuing, and commits therein many grievous sins: behold him, therefore, already well-nigh sold to hell! O miserable relatives, O unhappy friends, who in truth are cruel enemies, what is it that you do? Oh, how terrible a judgment awaits you at death! Is it not also a surprising thing to see incumbents, who are desirous of exchanging their benefices, inquiring of friends and looking about for some one with whom to effect the transaction, the only point dwelt upon being the amount of revenue they want? "I must have," they will say, "a benefice of two hundred crowns a year, a thousand crowns, more or less:" this is the first and main object. But alas! are they at any trouble to find a person, the worthiest among the worthy, that they may entrust the benefice to his hands? Of course I allow that when men have some fear of God, they say, "I want a good person; he must be one who is free from vice and lives respectably;" but as for considering anxiously whether he is possessed

moreover of supernatural talents, or leads a life more
than ordinarily edifying, more disengaged from the
world, more dead to earthly things, such as ecclesiastics ought to lead—alas! these things are not
thought of at all. O my God, how little is Thy
cause considered in this world!

CHAPTER IX.

JESUS HIDDEN AS TO HIS GRACES.

TRULY it is an extraordinary, an unexampled grace,
that a man should be at the same time both on the
way and at the term—that he should be at the same
time, to use theological terms, *viator* and *comprehensor*.
This privilege was reserved to our dear Jesus. But
what displays in an ineffable manner the love which
this God-Man ever bore to the hidden life, is that He
never suffered the glory of the beatific vision, which
He enjoyed without interruption in the supreme part
of His soul, to communicate itself, as it would have
done, to His body. But this is not all. If He must
needs let some rays of that beatific glory diffuse
themselves over His body for a very short space of
time, He does it in secret, in a secluded spot, and in
presence of only three of His disciples, and bids them
not to speak of it to any one whatever till after His
death, conversing with them thereof, and of the ignominies with which it should be attended; as if He
wished by this discourse to divert their thoughts from
His glory, and to fill their minds with the humiliation
and opprobrium of the cross.

We may say still more, and this it is that is infinitely adorable. What grace is equal to that of the hypostatic union? Can you by the widest range of thought, by the farthest stretch of imagination, conceive anything greater? Assuredly this grace surpasses all the conception of men and angels. Figure to yourself a soul united personally to a God—a man with a divine, not a human personality: such is Jesus in His admirable estate. What so transporting as this unspeakable grace? And yet the Holy Soul of Jesus not only derives therefrom no vain complacency, but keeps it hidden in a manner sufficient to fill the whole court of heaven with astonishment. The Eternal Father causes His voice to be heard on Thabor, declaring Jesus to be His Well-Beloved Son; and Jesus makes as though He heard it not, that He may converse on the ignominy of His Passion. It is related by St. Mark that at another time a voice was heard from heaven, declaring also that Jesus was the Well-Beloved Son of the Eternal Father; and this Evangelist tells us that immediately afterwards He retired into the wilderness (i. 11, 12).

O my Divine Master, O my Lord and my God, how dost Thou teach Thy creatures by Thy example to court obscurity. What instance can be found of so strong a love for a retired life, a life which remains shut up within itself, satisfied to have for its witness God alone, without exhibiting itself to creatures? How does a life so divine annihilate all the covert, subtle pretexts of self-love, whereby it seeks to induce souls to make known the graces they have received, and to talk about them. An important lesson to such directors as are too ready to draw attention to persons under their guidance, speaking of their grace and making others acquainted with them, for the purpose of attracting the esteem and friendship of men. Such conduct is often a great injury to the persons thus made the object of attention; it gives the devils a vantage ground against them; it detracts much from the purity of the grace they possess, and, by consequence, from their pure love of God only and of His glory. Oh, how blessed is the soul which is known of none! blessed the soul that falls into the hands of a director who keeps it quite concealed, who never speaks of it, nor allows it to speak about itself; who not only does not show the writings of those under his guidance, but prohibits them from writing, preserving them entirely for God alone, who ought to be sufficient for them; yes, God only, God only, God only, nothing more, nothing else! I do not mean by this to countenance in any way those directors who desire to attach souls to themselves, and who refuse them the liberty of laying open their interior to experienced servants of God, out of a jealousy which is not of God, but of man, and the self-love natural to him. Of this error I have spoken in my book entitled, "The Kingdom of God in Mental Prayer." I allude to those who bring them forward without any real necessity, and before indifferent persons. I am aware there are certain souls to whom it is useful to write down the graces they receive; but, in truth, this is of very rare occurrence: the danger is greater than is imagined, and we cannot employ too much caution in the matter, particularly in the case of the weaker sex, who are too much disposed to vanity.

I declare that when I consider the conduct of a God-Man, I do not understand how we can with so much readiness divulge the graces we have received. I allow there have been holy men and holy women who acted thus on occasions, but they did so by a special movement of the Holy Spirit, who designed to make use of such publication for His glory. This is why we ought scrupulously to refrain from condemming those servants of God who sometimes speak with simplicity of what passes in their interior, or of what has happened to them from without. For who can tell whether it be by a movement of nature or of grace that they speak, and disclose the merciful goodness of God in their regard? And who are we that we should judge the consciences of others? He who truly possesses the Spirit of God will not be forward in censuring the conduct of his neighbour, a fault of very great magnitude among spiritual persons. But judge well of every one, honouring all men, and humbling yourself below every being in the world without any exception.

I do not mean, then, to condemn any one in particular, but I simply say in a general way that the strong and tender affection which the Adorable Jesus bore to the hidden life, ought to inspire us with an extreme love for it. Were ever graces equal to those of this Amiable Saviour? And yet what greater care could He have taken to keep them concealed? If we contemplate closely the precious life of His most holy Mother, we shall observe the same affections and the same preferences. These admirable examples have had so powerful an effect on saints that they have desired nothing so earnestly as to keep themselves hidden. What have they not done to prevent their graces being known? How profound and how complete was the silence they kept in all that concerned those graces, or could attract the esteem of men ! Oh, what great things did the Lord work in them, which through this secresy of theirs will never be known ! Sufficient for them that God alone knows them; it is He only whom they sought to please. The glorious St. Ignatius, founder of the Company of Jesus, used to say that all the admirable things we read of in the Lives of Saints are nothing as compared with the marvels of grace which were wrought in the interior of their souls, and of which we possess no knowledge. Often even they employed a thousand holy artifices in order to try to conceal so much as we have been able to learn about them. It was necessary to have recourse to all sorts of measures, to labour hard and take great pains, in order to discover as much as we have been able to learn. Often, if some word about the graces they had received escaped them, they would instantly blush and be covered with confusion, as evidently feeling it a sensible mortification. More than this : they begged God not to give them such extraordinary graces as became apparent, as raptures and ecstacies, the gift of miracles, and such like things. They resisted with humility when they were granted them; they performed a number of devotions in order to prevail on the Divine Goodness to withdraw them; and sometimes God, in kindness to them, mercifully granted their request. For, indeed, it is a great mercy to possess nothing which can make us appear of any consequence in the eyes of men. However, we must beware of concealing anything that passes in our interior from a discreet director ; for otherwise we should expose ourselves to the delusions of the malignant spirit and to the deceits of nature. We must be thus unreserved because it is the will of God, renouncing all subtle and secret desire of our director's good opinion, in whom, as in all others, we must seek but God only. This is why those persons fail grievously who, having by the Divine assistance rid themselves of all attachment to the esteem and friendship of creatures, make a secret reservation in favour of their director, which they betray by their anxiety or fear lest they should not be sufficiently thought of by him: a fear which sometimes prevents them from fully laying open to him all their failings, or some particular faults into which they have fallen. The only reason, therefore, why we must inform our director of the graces we have received, is because it is the will of God. We must not waste time in long and frequent interviews without sufficient cause; such interviews are often a mere indulgence of nature and the occasion of disedification. He who will content himself with what is simply necessary, will know how to retrench everything superfluous in all such conferences.

CHAPTER X.

JESUS HIDDEN AS TO HIS DIVINE MISSION.

WHAT mission was ever like to that of the Adorable Jesus? Where is the mind, whether human or angelic, that can conceive anything more exalted and more divine? And its results again,—are they not altogether admirable? He who sends is a God: He is the Eternal Father. He who is sent is a God: He is the Well-Beloved Son of the Father. He who is given to carry on this divine mission is a God: He is the Holy Spirit.   She who of all pure creatures has the greatest share therein is the Mother of God: she is the most holy Virgin.   This mission regards not a few provinces or a few kingdoms, but the whole habitable earth, and all the men that dwell therein without exception.   Its object is to deliver from evils that are infinite, to bestow goods that shall endure for ever.   It is to make men gods by a participation of the divine nature; thus exalting in an incomparable manner even the most abject of men to an unimaginable glory, far above all that is greatest in this visible world ; for all the blessed inhabitants of Paradise will be mighty kings, the splendour of whose crowns and everlasting empire will be so marvellous that no mind can conceive their magnificence.

Nothing, then, can exceed the glory of a mission so noble and so divine.   But, O my amiable Saviour, most justly didst Thou say that Thou soughtest not Thine own glory ; Thou referrest it all to Thy Eternal Father, reserving to Thyself nothing but confusion and ignominy in this visible world.   Thou openest Thy mission in a poor stable, between two brute animals.   Thou commencest it with a flight full of disgrace in the world's judgment, an exile into a foreign land ; and Thou dost continue it in the dull obscurity of a poor carpenter's workshop.   Thy public preaching lasts but three years and a little more, and that amidst contradiction, envy, persecution, insult, calumny, and cruel hatred.   And in the end Thou bringest it to a close upon a gibbet between two thieves ; Thou dost finish it on a cross, which serves Thee for a pulpit from whence to preach Thy last sermon ; there Thou hangest, all naked and pierced with thorns and nails.   And in this state it is that all is consummated, and Thy mission is fulfilled. Thou wilt not behold during the days of Thy earthly pilgrimage the wondrous things it shall bring to pass; it is Thy will that these great and divine marvels should be wrought by Thy disciples! Ah! my good Master, I cannot weary of recounting Thy excessive love for the hidden life; and how, then, can we weep enough over the blindness of men, who do all they can to put themselves forward and get themselves known? Jesus discourses, exhorts, preaches—preaches divinely —and gains to His Father but a scanty number of souls; at the end of His life even these all abandon Him, and the faith—such is St. Bernard's opinion— scarcely survives save in the heart of the most holy Virgin. O marvel of marvels! Jesus leaves the earth, He finishes His mission; and at the conclusion of all His labours, the greatest that ever were known —the labours of a Man-God—He beholds scarcely more than one person who possesses fully the gift of faith. O human arrogance, O poor proud man, how ought this to abash and confound thee, who desirest always to succeed in thy designs, and art vexed when thou perceivest that they produce no great effect! Let us ever bear in mind the holy conduct of our good Master, who neglects nothing, yea, does every-thing, to teach us to renounce the inclinations of corrupt nature, which is ever urging us to put our-selves forward and court the world's esteem.

This Divine Master said (John xiv. 12) that His disciples should do greater things than He. And, indeed, He preached but for a few short years, during His mortal life, and then only in Judea and Galilee; but His disciples shall preach from one end of the world to the other, their voice shall be heard through all the earth. They shall destroy idolatry, they shall establish the worship of the true God, even unto the ends of the earth: they shall overthrow the dominion of the devil. A single one of His disciples, St. Francis Xavier, shall preach in four-and-twenty kingdoms, and shall baptize millions of persons, among whom will be found even crowned heads. Well do I know that it is Jesus who operates in all these things, seeing that He works by His disciples all the good that is done; but at the same time I know that He did not wish to enjoy these great and splendid successes during His earthly pilgrimage; for " verily He is a Hidden God."

How does such an example put to confusion those pitiful men who are not satisfied if their missions do not succeed as they expect; if their sermons produce little effect; if they meet with opposition and contradiction; if they are not much listened to, or followed, or applauded; if, instead of pleasing the popular taste, they are treated with contempt! Pitiful men! who desire to appear in conspicuous pulpits, to have the fashionable world present at their sermons, to preach in large towns, to deliver important courses of lectures, to be listened to by crowds of people, and alas! who sometimes solicit, sue, beg, intreat, intrigue for the occupation of some distinguished pulpit. Oh, how rare is that faith which imitates the conduct and life of Jesus our God! Do we really believe what we profess to believe? Have we faith in those great truths which we preach?

They who are truly imbued with the Spirit of God enter into the dispositions of Jesus their Head, the Life of their lives, the Soul of their souls. They sigh only after the hidden life; they would be known of no one; they have a horror of the vain distinctions of this world. Oh, how far removed are they from the desire of putting themselves forward by means of preaching or direction, employments which they never undertake except in submission to the command of God, as it is manifested to them by obedience, nor exercise except with fear; liking not the distractions they occasion, enduring with much repugnance the honour thence accruing, and avoiding with all possible care everything that can bring them into notice. If they occupy conspicuous pulpits, it is but to make known Jesus Christ, and Him only; what distresses them is to attract notice to themselves; their delight is to preach in country districts to poor people, or in obscure localities far away from the great world. Not but what their joy would indeed be great to see Jesus known and loved by all mankind, and for this it is that they speak and preach; but for themselves, they would be delighted to have no other portion than shame and confusion, in imitation of their dear Master and gracious Saviour.

They are filled with a holy envy of those Apostolic men who, instead of applauses, have met with nothing but reproaches, contempt, and insult. They believe firmly that doctrine of a God-Man—that blessed are we when men revile us and speak all that is evil against us; when they hate us, pursue us, persecute us, and even put us to death. They are not eager to acquire graceful manners, brilliant accomplishments, means of ingratiating themselves with persons of consideration, nor, what is pitiful to the last degree, and inspires the mind with horror, facilities of attaining important offices, rich benefices, and the highest dignities of the Church. They take but little trouble abo any temporal emoluments their employments may yield; they avoid all the honour and glory attendant upon them; they count everything but as dust and smoke, looking solely to the interests of Jesus only.

They who truly have the Spirit of God abandon to Him, without the least shadow of reservation, all the success of their designs, holding themselves in a state of perfect indifference with regard to consequences. They do everything which it is their duty to do with the divine assistance; they neglect nothing; they are generous in undertaking God's work, resolute in executing it, and steadfast in enduring the sufferings it entails; their perseverance never relaxes, their courage is indefatigable; all their stay being in God alone, they fear not what man or the devil can do unto them. Their strength is in the Name of the Lord, who hath made heaven and earth. They lift up their eyes unto the holy hills—the most holy Virgin, the good angels, and the saints—from whence they look for help; this done, they remain in undisturbed peace, whatever may betide. Moved as they are by the Spirit of God, their conduct truly reflects the divine ways. What does not God do for the salvation of man? And yet how few are saved! Does God on that account lose for a single instant His infinite peace? So is it with those who truly possess His Spirit. They do all that belongs to them to do by performing good works and persevering therein; if after this their good designs do not succeed, or at least have but little success, they are perfectly content; for though they desire what is good, they desire it in the way God wills it, and desire no more than God wills. It is self-love that is ever asking for great successes, and that brings trouble of mind, disappointment, vexation, dejection, weariness, and despondency when affairs do not prosper. Subtle in its self-seekings, it colours them with specious pretexts of virtue, desire for the perfection of souls, zeal for the glory of God; as if souls and the divine interests were not dearer to the Almighty than to the most zealous among men. Oh, how willingly does a pure soul commit to the hands of God all the issues of the holiest designs, losing not one whit of its tranquillity, let what will happen.

The thought of Jesus hidden while consummating the greatest work that ever was achieved, annihilates in us all selfish desires and engulphs them in the abyss of His infinite will, which we ought ever to adore, although it be beyond our understanding. He was pleased not to perform personally that which He wrought by His disciples, in order to teach us that the happiness of a Christian consists not in doing great things, but in doing what God wills we should do, nay, nothing at all, if it so pleases Him. The Son of God declares that there is no one among the children of men greater than John Baptist; and yet what external works did this angelic man perform? He spends almost all his life in the desert; he is seen only for a very short time on the banks of the Jordan; he never wrought a single miracle: this is a truth taught us by the Divine Word. If he reproves a profligate prince, his zeal produces so little effect in changing the life of the unhappy man whom he tries to reform, and is so ill received, that he is in consequence thrown into prison and loses his life. Woe to us, who, through a vicious self-love, hidden even from ourselves, are always desiring to be successful in whatever we undertake!

They who are really imbued with the Spirit of God, whenever He is pleased to bestow His benediction on their labours, endeavour to the utmost of their power to conceal the part they have in them. They do all they can to prevent any credit accruing to themselves therefrom, and feel an inexpressible joy when others reap the honour. Blessed state, which removes us from the sight and esteem of the creature; blessed, since it is the only means of our being noticed and esteemed by a God whose regard and esteem ought well to suffice us! O happy, a thousand times happy, they who labour meritoriously, but, through the Spirit of grace and by a special blessing, meet only with contradictions in the judgment of men, who censure and blame them. O happy they, whose occupations have nothing great in the world's eyes, and all the honour of which remains hidden and unperceived save by God alone! This precious grace is sometimes bestowed on directors of whom God makes great use, but in a secret way. God employs them in the guidance of certain souls eminent in sanctity, who glorify Him exceedingly, or for the conversion of sinners: but all this remains well-nigh unknown. It is bestowed also on certain preachers, who have only simple people for their hearers, or are but very little followed, but whom God favours with wonderful benedictions. For instance, a preacher has but fifty persons for his audience, and it pleases the all-good God to powerfully touch the hearts of thirty or forty of them: assuredly the effect of such a sermon is great in the eyes of God, although from the absence of numbers it is hidden from the eyes of men. It may happen, on the other hand, that a preacher may be listened to by two or three thousand

souls, who applaud and admire him and speak everywhere of his great talents: if out of this large
number of souls there are none who are converted
and amend their lives, or only some three or four,
in the sight of God the effects of grace are not to be
compared with the fruits gained by the other preacher
with his scanty audience, although in the eyes of the
world the one is hardly noticed in comparison with
the other. But the world, which has little spirituality
about it, regards only what is external and showy.
O my God, how different are Thy judgments from
those of men! This high grace, again, is bestowed
on certain souls destined to serve as victims to divine
justice for the sins of others. God, in consideration
of these souls, bestows the grace of conversion on a
large number of sinners, draws out of heresy and
infidelity many heretics and unbelievers, and sanc-
tifies many souls eminent in the path of virtue: yet
all this is hidden from the eyes of men, who are
ignorant of the heavy crosses which Divine Providence lays upon them for this end, or, if they know
them, understand not the grace nor the purpose for
which they are given. Who, on beholding the people
of God fighting and winning a glorious victory over
their enemies, would ever have thought that so great a
triumph was the effect of the prayers of a single man,
Moses, the servant of God? Who would not have
ascribed the glory to the strength and valour of the
warriors of the people of Israel? How true it is
that in the day of judgment many will be known
to have wrought great achievements within the
dominions of Christ's kingdom, who passed for in-
significant and useless persons in the world, and were
held in no repute even amongst good men. And as

true it is, that the great and wonderful deeds of many which made so much noise and rendered those who wrought them so famous, will be found empty, full of the self-seekings of nature, and devoid of the Spirit of God.

I will conclude this chapter by relating what is told of Father De Condren, one who was eminent for his love of the hidden life. This holy man, who desired but God alone, being engaged in important matters, most glorious to God and the Church, and advantageous to the State, and having laboured at them most meritoriously and with great blessing on his efforts, when he saw they were on the point of being known to the world, transferred them by a holy artifice to the hands of others, that, their successful issue being attributed to them, these persons might gain an honour which after God and in God was due to himself, and that no one might have so much as the slightest thought of him whom God had employed to bring affairs of so much importance to a prosperous termination through his diligence and exertions. Oh, how far removed is such conduct from that of people who are so ready to talk of the share they have had in great matters ; who are delighted when others think and speak of it ; who are annoyed when no one notices their labours, or the good that has resulted from them ; who are pained if others receive the credit due to themselves; who like to perform their good works conspicuously, and are the first to put themselves forward and converse with persons of rank who take an interest in these works—to see them and be seen of them; who would be mortified if people did not consult them and employ them and attend their charitable meetings ; who wish to be thought the leading persons in such benevolent works! O my God, how much is there of the creature everywhere and how rare is it to find God only anywhere! God only, God only, God only!

CHAPTER XI.

JESUS HIDDEN EVEN WHEN MOST SEEN.

THAT great servant of Jesus Christ, Father De Condren, used to say that in our Saviour there was a life so holy and so withdrawn into God His Father, that, though men heard His words and saw His actions, no mind was ever able to comprehend the closeness of His application to God. So true it is that He remained always hidden even in His most notable actions, and that what was most divine and greatest in Him was unknown to men. This is why His faithful servant of whom I have just spoken, used to teach that we ought to live more in what is secret to us, and in the hidden dispositions of our Lord, than in what has been positively made known to us.

But we must again remark upon the very astonishing predilection which the Adorable Jesus showed for the hidden life during the years in which He lived in public and conversed with men. It was His delight to pass whole nights in prayer in secluded spots; if He sees Himself surrounded by a multitude, He withdraws and escapes into the mountains; if He would repose from His labours, He retires into the desert. He keeps aloof from towns and large assemblies ; He enjoins silence on those who witness His greatest miracles. If He goes into the Garden of Olives, to suffer there an agony inexpressible, He takes with Him but three of His disciples ; and again He separates Himself even from them, that His Father alone may behold His exceeding sorrows. True it is that on Thabor He manifested some rays of His glory, but observe : it is in a place apart, and, His mind and heart being all the while on Calvary, He discourses only on the ignominies of His Passion. It would seem as if He wished to veil the brilliancy of His glories with the intensity of His humiliations. Moses and Elias appear with Him on this holy mountain, and, instead of descanting with admiration and astonishment on the splendour, the beauty, and the glory of the Adorable Jesus, they are occupied only with the dreadful sufferings of His cross, and speak of nothing else. Jesus Himself (as has been already remarked) seems desirous, by discoursing immediately afterwards on the shame and ignominies of His death, to remove from the minds of His most favoured Apostles the memory of what they had seen. Striking lesson for such souls as are favoured with extraordinary graces, not to make them known or speak about them except when necessity requires, as in the case of directors, but to conceal them as much as possible by laying open defects calculated to humble them in the eyes of others. Jesus fills the mind and the memory of His beloved Apostles with the thought of His shame ; He would have them occupied with His disgrace and ignominy ; while we can scarcely endure to have our humiliations spoken of, and are miserable at their being dwelt upon or thought of.

Alas! how few are there who choose for the subject of their conversation what may cause them shame and confusion.

We must observe also that the most conspicuous actions of the Son of God were hidden in the exceeding humiliations that followed. Never was preaching so divine, but all the glory that ought to have resulted from it was clouded by the scorn that was cast upon it, as is related in the Gospels; His very kindred condemning it, and regarding Him as a madman who, having lost his reason, required to be kept under restraint. Let those who desire the approbation of creatures come hither and learn from the example of their Master what result they ought to expect from their good works. It is sufficient to please God only, and we never please Him more than when we please creatures least. Woe to those who are applauded by the world! for the great Apostle assures us (Gal. i. 10) that, if he pleased men, he should not be the servant of Jesus Christ. Oh, how little do men know what they say, when they rate so highly the condition of those who are admired, esteemed, and loved by all the world! How do they deceive themselves, who labour with so much eagerness to please creatures! Blessed is he whose life is conformable to the life of Jesus and that of His saints; who has had no lack of crosses, or of the contempt, the desertion, and the persecution of men! O state more enviable than we are prone to think! How great will be their confidence at the hour of death who have had no share in the esteem and friendship of creatures! With what joy will they depart from a world to which they never belonged! With what longing desire will they appear in the presence of the Lord whom only they have loved! But with what grief and anguish will the lovers of the world quit the object of their love! What pain to be torn away from that to which they are attached by ten thousand dreadful cords and chains! With what terror will they find themselves in the presence of a God of whom they have thought so little; whom they have served so ill and offended so much! No, it is difficult to be happy both in this world and in the other; this is why nothing gives sweeter, stronger, and more solid hopes of the happiness of another life than the miseries of the present, if we do but use them in a Christian way; and, on the other hand, I know of nothing which inspires so great a dread of an unhappy eternity than the joys, the pleasures, the goods, the honours, and the satisfactions of the present time. "My son," said Abraham to the wretched rich man in hell, "remember that thou didst live in ease and abundance during thy mortal life, and that, if Lazarus possesses now the happiness which those enjoy who are in the friendship of God, he had in past time sorrows and sufferings for his portion while he was in the world." Oh, how far better to suffer humiliations at the hands of men in company with Jesus Christ, who is everywhere contemned and contradicted! If He makes known who He is, they seek to stone Him. If He confesses that He is the Son of God, they spit in His face, they buffet Him. If He puts devils to flight, if He displays his empire over hell, they accuse Him of a secret complicity with Beelzebub. If He teaches souls the way of eternal happiness, they cry out against Him as a deceiver of the people. In truth, is He not marvellously hidden, even when He shows Himself the most?

CHAPTER XII.

JESUS HIDDEN IN HIS GLORIOUS LIFE.

JESUS, knowing that creatures are prone to put themselves forward in all things—some of purpose and design and with manifest knowledge of what they do, others through a subtle and almost imperceptible self-seeking; some in temporal things, others, who have renounced mere material aims, in spiritual things, and even such are most divine—and knowing, on the other hand, the infinite greatness of His Eternal Father, who ought to be the supreme object of regard in everything, and that in strict justice He alone ought to be magnified in all, it being the part of creatures to remain in their own nothingness—Jesus, I say, in order to satisfy the justice of His Father, offended by so monstrous a perversion, hides Himself in an infinitely astonishing manner, and endures annihilations at which we stand aghast. O my good Saviour, O my God, what a lesson dost Thou give to our proud and self-sufficient minds !

Alas ! it is but too true ; we are ever wishing to hold a place in the mind and heart of creatures, and to be esteemed and loved by them, although their minds and hearts ought to be filled but with God alone. And thus it is we dispute with a God for what belongs exclusively to Him. Father De Condren, who was sensibly penetrated with this truth, travelling while very young, perhaps about seventeen or eighteen years of age, as he was passing by an inn, overheard a servant-maid say, alluding to him, "What well-made boots that young gentleman has on." Seized on the moment with a zeal all divine, he cut the heel off one of them in order to spoil its appearance. "O my God," cried the youth, whom we may justly characterize as heavenly-minded, "is it possible that I can allow such a thing as a boot to occupy the mind of a creature who ought to think but of God alone ?"

And yet men, such is their inexplicable blindness, are far indeed from performing such Christian acts. We have said, and it cannot be sufficiently repeated, that they are always wishing to be objects of attention, and are distressed when they are not so. And what will they not do in order to occupy a place in the minds and hearts of creatures ? If they converse, if they write, if they engage in affairs, if they hold any office, all their desire is to be noticed. There is not one, down to the poorest artizan, the labourer, or the vine-dresser, the meanest person on the face of the earth, who does not court the world's good opinion. If we are building a house, or are engaged in any other work, if we are dressing, in short, in everything, however trifling, we are always wishing to distinguish ourselves. Thus it is that most creatures occupy themselves and occupy others. There are few who endeavour, with the divine assistance, to empty themselves of every created thing, and to take up no room in souls which ought to be full of God only, who desire in all things to be nothing, that in all things God alone may dwell, and live, and reign. This it is that constrained the Adorable Jesus to annihilate Himself, as the divine word declares. A worm of the earth, a very nothing, disputes pre-eminence with a being supremely, infinitely adorable—a God. Jesus, to repair this wrong, Very God as He is, hesitates not to sacrifice Himself to His Father by an annihilation such as an eternity will never be able sufficiently to admire. He annihilates Himself by becoming man, to use the language of the divine Paul; He annihilates Himself on the cross, surrendering there the most precious of lives; and in the mysteries both of His Birth and of His Death He is, after an ineffable manner, the Hidden God. But this is not all: foreseeing that the creature will always desire to make itself of importance, He resolves to annihilate Himself even to the consummation of ages, in order to display the sovereignty of His Father, the One Infinite Being; so that it would be true to say that, all glorious as He is in the height of heaven, seeing that He is there the object of the adoring love of Paradise, He is more than ever hidden on this earth of ours.

O the supremely adorable greatness of my God! My heart and my flesh faint at the contemplation of it. I lose myself in an unfathomable abyss. Ah! my soul, my soul, art thou not covered with confusion? Whither can we flee? Where can we hide ourselves? Where shall we find humiliations deep enough to plunge into? Can we ever annihilate ourselves enough? After what we have seen shall we still have the hardihood to exalt ourselves? Can there still remain in us the slightest disposition to engage the hearts of creatures, yea but for an instant? Is not the thought itself intolerable? Shall we not make our life one unceasing sacrifice and oblation, devoting, immolating all to the Sovereign Greatness of the Infinite Being of a God? Shall we not conceive the most ardent love, the most insatiable desire, for the hidden life? Shall we not long to live unknown among men, as though we were not in existence? Or, if our existence be known, let us at least sink into nothing, like worthless persons, wretched criminals, broken and crushed by the contradiction of the world, contempt, calumny, and every manner of cross.

Come, all ye creatures, come in crowds, to contemplate the life of Jesus hidden even in His state of glory; and then consider what you ought to do, and what you ought to cease from doing, be your condition what it may. I will but say one word on what I have discussed at large in two of my little works: one entitled "The Love of our Lord Jesus Christ," the other "The Love of Jesus in the Most Holy Sacrament of the Altar." Briefly, then, I will say, that Jesus in His state of glory does not appear merely as a little child, as He did in the manger; or as a man, as He did on Calvary; but, O infinite wonder! abiding with us on this earth of ours in the Divine Eucharist, He appears therein no more than if He were absent altogether. He remains hidden there under the appearance of bread and wine, under the appearance of a crumb of bread and a drop of wine! Can He, I would ask, conceal Himself more perfectly? Assuredly it must be confessed that the love of this God-Man for the hidden life is most intense and most amazing. But in saying this, remember, O my soul, and never forget, that it is thy vain-glory, thy desire of being of importance and appearing of importance, and the same dispositions on the part of creatures like thyself, that caused these terrible annihilations of a God. After such a spectacle, shall we grieve at being left unnoticed or disregarded? O my good Saviour and my God, what is it Thou doest? to what a state dost Thou reduce Thyself? Truly it is to hide Thyself in an incomprehensible manner, thus to abide concealed under particles of bread, which sometimes, falling unperceived to the ground, lie in the dust of our churches, exposed to be trodden under foot of all who come. O my God, who could ever have imagined such a thing? Could angels, could the very seraphim, ever have conceived the slightest thought of a state so hidden, however great the lights with which they were endowed? Is there a creature, how vile soever it be, that is hidden in such wise? A worm of the earth, an ant, would be seen, would be perceptible where Thou canst not be discovered. O the Adorable Majesty of my God: a drop of water, a blade of grass, is visible to the eye, while He whom heaven and earth cannot contain is not to be discerned. O love! O love! O goodness! O the miracle of the unsearchable ways of the Almighty!

Oh, that men would at least acknowledge, by the help of divine grace, according to their poor ability, conduct so winning and so admirable! But, far from being as sensible of it as they ought, they make it an occasion of ingratitude, infidelity, and sin. Jesus hidden, even in His state of glory, in the Most Holy Sacrament of the Altar, gives occasion to the heretic, out of the very malice of his heart, to dispute His loving presence in that mystery : thus the heretic makes Him endure an exceeding annihilation by denying that He is present there at all. But what shall we say of those who call themselves Catholics, and profess to acknowledge the presence of Jesus in the Most Holy Sacrament of the Altar? They protest and declare that they are ready to seal this truth with their blood ; and, indeed, it is this assurance of faith on their part that makes their ingratitude appear all the more flagrant, carried as it is to an excess which it is difficult to conceive. For if we doubt not the presence of Jesus on our altars, and if we firmly believe that Jesus is God, how can we commit so many irreverences before His Divine Majesty? Alas ! what proofs do we give of our faith? Where is the unbeliever who could persuade himself that Catholics really believe in the Presence of God, when they see them so far removed from paying Him the homage which is His due ; when they mark those irreverent postures of theirs in the churches, those wandering eyes, attracted by everything that passes before them, the conversations they permit themselves, and all the useless words they say, that indecorous behaviour, that vanity of dress, and that immodest display on the part of women ; when they observe persons making their genuflexion only on one knee, or remaining covered, even when the Most Holy Sacrament is exposed, occupying themselves with wretched creatures, while their Creator is revealing Himself to them in so loving a manner, though veiled under the sacramental species ; when they see the insolent behaviour of servants, which so often occurs while they are keeping places for their masters, and the little care their masters take to remedy the evil, and the little zeal persons of every condition show in preventing all these profanations? Do such things as these speak highly for our faith? But if, after all, we persist in maintaining that nevertheless we do believe, then I ask how we can have the face to treat a Present God so unworthily? O the exceeding insensibility and ingratitude of creatures! If we are in the presence of a monarch, we are thoughtful enough of the honour which is due to him, and fail not to remember it. And there is no doubt if any one over whom we had authority were wanting in respectful behaviour, we should take care to correct him; a servant would soon be dismissed, and even chastised and punished, if he had neglected to show proper respect to the king's majesty, and, let me add, to any one possessed of the least degree of rank. It is God alone who is not considered; we pass very lightly over offences committed against His Divine Goodness; these are not things that lie nearest our heart. But let a footman or a maid-servant know how to please us, or make themselves necessary to us, and this will weigh more with us than the thought of the God whose service they neglect. O my God, O my God, how do men treat Thee! O Adorable Jesus, Thou abidest ever hidden even in Thy state of glory. But know, O men, that yet a little while and you must appear before His tremendous judgment-seat, and then will you learn what it is to have to deal with a God.

CHAPTER XIII.

JESUS HIDDEN IN HIS MOST HOLY MOTHER AND HIS SAINTS.

IT is not enough for the Adorable Jesus to remain hidden in His Person, in His states of life, and in His mysteries; He is pleased, moreover, to hide Himself in His most holy Mother and in His Saints; in everything that is most closely united with Him; in fine, in everything that belongs to Him, according to the multitude of His great mercies and the measure of His exceeding charity. The Son of God, consubstantial with His Father, resolves to descend from heaven upon earth, there to be made man; and to this end He chooses a virgin mother, in whom He is pleased to become incarnate. But, O the depth of the counsels of a God! He will have for His mother one who is poor, little considered among creatures, despised by the world, the wife of a poor artisan, a carpenter. I leave it to Christians to reflect, with the most profound attention, on this all-holy and all-divine conduct of our gracious Saviour. I invite them to meditate at their leisure on truths, uttered, indeed, in few words, little dwelt upon, and with which the generality of souls are but little penetrated, but which demand, not only all the days of our life, but a whole eternity, that they may be contemplated with all possible veneration, intelligence, and love. O my good Master, O my amiable Saviour, what dost Thou not do to teach mankind the Infinite Greatness of God Thy Father, and the nothingness of every created being! Oh, what an example dost Thou give us to hide ourselves in all things, that God alone may be manifested, known, and loved. Ah, love, the love of my Jesus, how admirable art thou! And Thy annihilations, O my Saviour, how great is their excess in everything! I behold Thee from the moment of Thy Divine Incarnation to the last instant of Thy precious life; I behold Thee in Thyself; I behold Thee in all Thy states, and in Thy mysteries; I behold Thee in all Thou sayest, all Thou doest; and I see that in all things and everywhere Thou seekest not Thine own glory, Thou takest not therein the least complacency, Thou referrest all to Thy Father, annihilating Thyself in His Divine Presence. I see, moreover, that Thou seekest these unspeakable annihilations in everything that concerns Thee, in everything that belongs to Thee. Certainly, after such a contemplation, we must remain convinced that in all Thou art, in all Thou doest, Thou lovingly expiatest the pretensions of creatures, who, though they are nothing, are ever desiring to be something, to the prejudice of Thy Sovereign Being. Let me here repeat, and repeat it with tears: Nothingness wishes to *be*, while the Great All annihilates Himself. O my soul, knowest thou what it is thou believest? Jesus, the Great All, annihilates Himself, not only in His Incarnation, in His Death, but for more than 1,700 years; and He will continue to do the same even to the consummation of the world, not only in some single province or kingdom, but in every place where there shall be an altar throughout the habitable earth. And, O my God, how many such places are there at this moment in the world ! He will endure without ceasing this 'state of annihilation before the Sovereignty of His Father, to appease His justice, so deeply incensed by the self-exaltation of creatures ; and creatures will never cease thus insolently to exalt themselves. This state of a Man-God, so infinitely astounding, will never win their hearts. Let a God-Man—I must repeat it—let a God-Man hide Himself as much as He will, the worm of the earth, that wretched nonentity, will continue to display itself to the utmost of its power. Truly the mind is lost in the contemplation. O my soul, are we speaking of illusions or of truths ? Ah ! doubt there is none, they are incontestable truths : and how can we survive the knowledge of them ? Oh, how justly have saints said that to enlightened souls life is an endurance, and death an object of longing desire !

And here I cannot pass over in silence the conduct of certain Christians, which to me can never be matter of sufficient astonishment. I allude to those families who have the Tremendous Sacrifice of the Mass offered in their private chapels, of which it is not too much to say that they are the least ornamented part of their houses. The furniture of their saloons and apartments is incomparably more beautiful ; the beds whereon miserable creatures take their rest are richer and more costly than that which is used to receive the Body of a God. We know by our own experience that people will scarcely go to the expense of a decent portable altar, most of those employed being too small or very shabby. We know how they will grudge a few corporals for the Body of a God, whilst their presses are full of fine linen for the use of their own bodies of corruption ; and, what is most shocking of all, we find sometimes chalices of pewter where there is no lack of silver for their own table.* What shall I say of the little reverence shown for these most holy places ? A lady exclaims if she perceives that her room is not perfectly clean, while the chapel is left full of dust. Care must be taken not to present her with anything but pure white linen, while the altar is served with napkins, albs, and corporals which have been used again and again without being washed. The key of the cabinet and the bureau is put away securely, while the key of the chapel is left unheeded, and shameful profanations— we say what we know—occur in consequence. Again, chapels are sometimes situated close to bed-rooms or apartments where play goes on, and a thousand silly things are said, and even many offences are committed. How many of these chapels are allowed to remain in such a state that you would rather suppose that unbelievers had the keeping of them than Catholics ! I do not mean by this to blame the use of private chapels, approved as it is by the permissions which bishops are in the habit of granting, but I deplore their abuse.

* That these reproaches were not without an immediate application among ourselves a few years ago, we are reminded by the following anecdote given in the recently published " Life of Mother Margaret " :—"Visiting at a great house, she was questioned by the ladies of the family as to what she thought of England after her long absence in a foreign country, ' Well, ladies,' she replied ; ' if I must say the truth, what has struck me most in England is to see you using mahogany for your closets, *whilst you keep our Lord in deal.'"

I protest that all these things show me, in a way I cannot express, how true it is that Jesus is a Hidden God. And for you, O creatures, do you reflect what it is you do? Alas! are you not satisfied with the annihilations which a God endures to atone for your self-exaltation? Must you even inflict fresh ones upon Him? I could not refrain from making this digression, feeling myself on the moment vividly affected by the thought of such treatment offered to my dear Master. Ah! how happy should I esteem myself if, reflecting on this, the hearts of some of the owners of these chapels should be moved to regard them as houses of the Living God, and to take such care of them as becomes persons who profess to have faith. Oh, how desirable it is that many should forego something of the comfort of private devotion, and go to hear the Most Holy Mass in the public churches, and not in their own domestic chapels; and so their use might become very rare, and be allowed only under extraordinary circumstances, and never without all the conditions which the order of the Church and the sanctity of the place and of the Divine Mysteries require. Oh, that man knew something of the Greatness of God! Woe unto us, clods of the earth as we are, who treat so familiarly and with so little respect an Infinite Majesty, before which the powers of the heavens tremble. Far better often would it be to abstain from hearing the Holy Mass, when we are prevented leaving home, than, under pretence of assisting thereat, to behave to a God as we behave to Him! Fain would I go and cry through the whole earth, "O men, O men, learn what my God is; know once for all that He is infinitely great and infinitely terrible." Holy Church sings in astonishment, that when He was pleased to be made man He "did not abhor the Virgin's womb." What will become of you, you who call Him down into your domestic chapels, so meanly adorned, so unbecomingly situated, and of which you take so little care? Hearken, O miserable creatures, yet a little while, yet a little while, and you will learn the Infinite Greatness of my God; but alas! it is a knowledge which will then come too late; you will have a whole eternity wherein to ponder it at your leisure.

I return to the subject of this chapter, and I say that the God of all glory was pleased to be hidden even in His holy Mother, and in all who were connected with Him; seeing that He chose a poor woman for His mother, a carpenter for His reputed father, and fishermen for His apostles. The holy Gospel teaches us that this very thing was made matter of reproach to Him, and that they who heard Him preach said, as St. Matthew informs us (xiii. 55), and as we have already observed, "Is not this the carpenter's son? Is not his mother called Mary?" And St. Mark tells us (vi. 3) that they said, "Is not this the carpenter, the son of Mary?" O the adorable conduct of a God-Man, who by His example effectually destroys all the excuses and vain pretexts of men! What now will say those preachers, those ministers, those directors, those ecclesiastical or religious persons, who still continue to set a value on their worldly rank, and sometimes under the plea of effecting some good by it? Assuredly, my God and Master knew well the true worth of things, He understood what measures to take, and yet how far removed is He from any such human views! Learn, O ye Christian men and women, to moderate this desire of being distinguished for your birth, and beware you do not lose your souls for the sake of some point of honour, of which that birth is the pretence. Oh, the atrocious, the horrible wickedness of those men who kill each other in duels, or who engage in miserable quarrels, all arising from disputes about this accursed point of honour, and who sometimes proceed to such an excess of impiety and fury, as not even to spare the august sanctity of our churches, and the very Presence of God, who will judge them and who dwells bodily therein. Accursed and wretched creatures, who are the occasions of these things, and who cause the eternal damnation of those who ought to be dearest to you ! You will see, you will see in hell, what this point of honour will avail you ; you will see with what consideration the devils will treat you on account of your rank and precedence in the world, and what deference they will show you in that place of torment. Learn, O Christians, not to be ashamed of your poor relations, if you have any ; not to distress yourselves if you are destitute of worldly rank ; or if, appearing of some consideration among men, they come to know that you are of inferior or low condition. And should you possess any advantages of birth, shrink from priding yourself upon it, or speaking often of it, or seeking occasion to make others allude to it. But of this fault we have already treated in the second chapter of this first part.

Let us return to the consideration of our gracious Saviour hidden in everything that most intimately appertains to Him. He was hidden in His religion, which was a stumbling-block to the Jews and appeared foolishness to the Gentiles. We may say more : it was held in such detestation by the wise men of the world, that never was persecution heard tell of like that which it endured.   Let any one read of the sufferings, the torments, the agonies, of the glorious martyrs of this holy religion, and there is no reasonable mind but must assent to the truth of this assertion.   But this is not all.   Who could have imagined that all that is best and most divine in His religion would lie hidden even from those who glory in following His laws and who profess the Catholic faith ? Yet experience leaves us only too certain of the fact.   Is it not true that it is rare to find among the faithful, persons who appreciate His holiest maxims of poverty, contempt, and suffering ? Is it not true that the purity of His doctrine is still persecuted by many Catholics ?   Let Apostolic men mention or even suggest Christian self-renunciation, detachment from the world, contempt of riches, pure love of sufferings, the nothingness of creatures, and people will scarcely endure to listen to them : they turn away from them with scorn, contradict them, and raise a thousand difficulties.   But what is strangest of all, is to see that devotion either frightens persons from practising it, or makes them ashamed of professing it, or serves only as a subject of mockery and contempt.   There are some so little enlightened, that they fancy they should pass a miserable existence if they embraced a devout life.   Others there are who have a certain amount of devotion, but are what we may call secret disciples : they take good care to give no token of it in public ; they tell you they wish their devotion to be all interior.   I know very well that we must not make an exhibition of anything extraordinary.   If we take the discipline, or practise unusual austerities, or wear a hair-shirt, or perform remarkable acts of charity, and other like things, we ought to keep such practices secret. But to be afraid to say that we aspire to devotion; that we desire to follow Jesus Christ according to the rules of the Gospel; that His maxims only are true, that the maxims of the world are deceitful, and the world itself deceived; that we profess to live as Christians and not as men of the world,—this it is that is intolerable. It is to be ashamed of Jesus Christ and of His Gospel; it is to be ashamed of the God whom we adore, if we are ashamed of being devout. But this blindness goes much farther, since it proceeds even to cast ridicule on devotion. You will see, not Pagans, not Turks, but Christians, Catholics, making devotion and devout people the object of their derision and scorn.

And here I would ask every reasonable mind to reflect a little and consider two things: devotion as it is in itself, and devotion as it is practised by certain persons who make it consist in what it does not consist in, or who are not free from many defects, or are guilty of many faults. If we consider devotion in itself, it is nothing else but the promptitude of a will resolutely bent upon serving God and doing whatever is pleasing to Him. It does not mean simply some love of God, but an eminent love; so that to aspire to devotion is to aspire to the service and love of the Sovereign of all things; truly to practise devotion is to perform His commands, to fulfil His divine will with courage, and generosity, and promptitude. Now I ask, looking at the matter in the true light in which we ought to regard it, what reasonable person is there who will say that he does

not aim at being devout, or who will not venture to
declare that he makes profession of devotion, or who
will be so impious as to make a mock of it?   For
how can a man—I do not say a Christian, but a
Turk, any man who acknowledges there is a God—
assert that he does not, at the least, aspire to serve
Him and to do His will?   Or how can he be ashamed
of the service of so adorable a Majesty?   How can
he make it a subject of sport and derision?   I
know that it will be said to me that it is not the
service of God which people are ashamed of, or which
they make the subject of ridicule.   But if devotion
is nothing else but the promptitude of a will devoted
to the service of God—a will, not only bent on
serving Him, but on serving Him with fervour and
generosity—to say that it is not the service of God of
which we are ashamed and of which we make a mock,
when we ridicule and are ashamed of devotion, is what
cannot be maintained by any one with the slightest pretension to being accounted a reasonable being.   I add,
that if devotion includes, not only a faithful obedience
to the commands of God, but also a generous love of
whatever concerns His glory, is it possible to find
creatures—is it possible there ever could be found creatures—who are afraid of making an open and public
profession of serving their Creator generously and
nobly?   And yet this is what you do, when you dare
not profess devotion before the world and in good
society; when you say you make no pretension to
being devout—that you are not one of those people
who want to be saints.   I entreat you to recollect
yourselves a little, and think what it is you say.   For
myself, I must confess that I am struck with fear, and
tremble at the very thought.   What! would you

venture to treat a king or some great one of the earth in this way?—nay, I might say, a friend, any one for whom you had the slightest respect? If you had to make him some protestation of service, would you do it only in secret and by stealth? and would you say in his very presence that you had no intention of serving him to the best of your power? No, a creature would not put up with conduct so base, and must a God endure it from you? O dreadful perversion of all sound reason! No one would dare to treat a miserable creature as the Creator of the Universe is treated. Ah! what will you say to Him when you behold Him in the majesty of His glory?. Know you not that the Adorable Jesus will not acknowledge in the presence of His Father those who are ashamed of Him before the world? We account it an honour to be in the service of kings and princes : we talk of it, publish it abroad, boast of it; and how many courtiers are there who are ready to suffer anything or do anything to enjoy a like distinction! It is Thou only, O King of kings, before whom all the monarchs of the earth are but as dust and nothingness —Thou only who art made of no account. O my Lord, how art Thou treated in this world below! What, then, must we think of those who add mockery to cowardice; who not only are ashamed of being thought devout, but laugh at devotion in others? Hear, O ye heavens, and give ear, O earth; hearken to this lump of clay. Devotion is one and the same thing with an eminent love of God. To scoff at devotion, therefore, is to throw contempt on a true and fervent love of God. Is this conceivable? Canst thou thyself conceive it who art guilty of it?

Some one may still answer me and say—for a disorderly love of self does not want for excuses—that it is not so much devotion which people are ashamed of, and which they ridicule, as certain practices of devotion. But I would beg these persons to examine with me in detail the practices they dislike, that the mouth of iniquity may be for ever stopped, and the self-invented delusions in which it indulges, to its own destruction, may be laid bare before its eyes. These, then, are the practices of devotion : to regulate the exterior carefully ; to be content with neat and modest apparel ; not to endure that shameful custom of exposing the arms and neck ; to maintain a well-ordered but reasonable establishment ; to spend what is necessary, according to our state, but to avoid all extravagance ; to pay and receive such visits as are suitable to our condition, but to observe all moderation therein ; to take needful recreation ourselves, and provide the same for our family, but not to waste time in useless and idle occupations ; to have fixed hours for giving ourselves to prayer and meditation on Christian truths, but so as not to interfere with the proper attention we ought to pay to our household affairs, acquitting ourselves faithfully of the obligations of our state, as God has ordered them, and of the duties and cares that belong to it ; to be amiably sociable when in company, behaving with the cheerfulness and the decorous gaiety becoming a Christian, bearing with the ill-humour of others, using condescension, always preserving a gentle and equal temper, and withal never departing from a modest reserve ; tolerating no foolish flattery, or the slightest familiarity which could in any way offend modesty, or words of double meaning, or jesting on religion, or oaths, or backbiting, or ridicule of others ; never indulging in any amusement which may be the occasion of displeasing God or scandalizing our neighbour; never entering into coteries, or forming dangerous connections and friendships, or such as tend to impair the spirit of piety. To practise devotion is to show honour to all, to offend none; to discharge our debts punctually; to pay our servants their due wages, and treat them with mildness; to behave ourselves peaceably in our own household, without scolding or brawling, bringing up our family with care, affection, and gentleness; rendering to husband or wife all the respect and all the love due to them, inducing a habit of mutual forbearance, joined to much patience and kindness. To practise devotion is to deal justly with every one; never to go to law except from pure necessity; never to defend ourselves but with regret; never to employ any power, credit, or influence we may possess to withhold from another what belongs to him; not to oppress those who are dependent on us; to take care that our tenants may be able to make a competent livelihood out of their farms, not letting them at too high a rent, considering the large unforeseen losses they are apt to incur, scrupulously respecting the rights of the poor as of the rich; to be on our guard against allowing our minds to be warped by self-interest, but dealing liberally with the needy. To practise devotion is to observe truth in our words; to shun deceit; to be frank and open in our conversation; to love our friends sincerely, and serve them generously; to love our very enemies, to speak well of them, and show kindness to them when occasion offers. To practise devotion is to comfort the afflicted; to assist with advice or money such as are in want; to visit hospitals and prisons, and do good to all men. And now I would ask what ground there is to be ashamed of devotion, and where we can find matter for ridicule and scoffing.

But let us proceed to examine other practices which furnish worldly people with further pretexts. It is true that devotion prompts us to speak of God and hear him spoken of with joy, to apply ourselves to the reading of spiritual books, to prayer and communing with God, and the different exercises of piety suitable to our vocation, and disposes us to the frequent use of the sacraments and the performance of other good works. It prompts us to labour with a holy zeal for the maintenance of all that concerns the worship of God, the decoration of churches, the promotion of pious works, and to leave no means untried to prevent whatever is opposed to the interests of our Sovereign Lord; as the reading of improper books, pernicious conversation in society, dangerous intercourse and friendships, oaths, slanders, quarrels, injustice, impurity, licentiousness. And these are the practices of which Christians are ashamed, and from which the libertine takes occasion for his scoffing! There are some who would scarcely venture to speak of God in company, for fear of passing for enthusiasts; who perform no exercises of piety except in secret, through dread of the world; who have not courage enough to take God's part when occasion offers; who would not dare to say a word to put a stop to profane swearing, familiarities, immodesties, irreverences committed in our very churches, or slanders against their neighbour. Pitiful people! who have not the boldness to open their mouth, or to do the least thing, in defence of the cause of the God whom they adore, and dare not even profess to belong to His devout worshippers,—that is to say, to those who serve Him in a more perfect way; whilst people of the world, and devout persons also, count it an honour and make it their glory and their boast to be in the service of the great ones of the earth, and every one boldly bestirs himself to defend their interests. One of the great men of the last century, Father Laynez, a companion of St. Ignatius, and his successor in the generalship of the Company of Jesus, used to say that the want of boldness and courage in speaking for God as occasion offered, was the cause of our greatest evils; and the reason is very plain: for is it not, in truth, conduct most unworthy of a God to be ashamed of Him before creatures, whilst creatures are bold in each other's defence? Yes, people may be seen gossiping and talking and acting most improperly in church; some bend only one knee before the Adorable Majesty of a God,* an abuse that has become very common, particularly in large towns; others behave unbecomingly—for instance, women and girls, with their immodest attire and conceited airs. But, alas! who thinks of raising his voice to vindicate the Majesty of God present on our altars?—who undertakes His cause? I have observed that such an occurrence is so rare—I noticed it only the other day, in one of the largest churches of France —that if any one ventures, however discreetly, to reprove those who commit such irreverences, people are quite astonished, and stare at him as at some extraordinary personage. O my God, O my God, O my Sovereign Lord, how deplorable! In the presence of the God who reposes on our altars, people have the

---

* That is to say, during Exposition of the Blessed Sacrament, *supra*, p. 66.

audacity to talk and converse about their affairs, and you will see groups of Christians discoursing and entertaining each other about things of the earth and the world, the news of the day, the veriest trifles; while scarcely will one person be found who dares to speak to these people in God's behalf, and recall them to themselves by some suitable reflections. O the excessive blindness of those who, having houses and public places to talk and converse in, come into our churches as though for the purpose of profaning them, and make those temples of propitiation and mercy the very storehouses of God's indignation and wrath against their souls. O Christians, again I ask, what are you thinking of? Do you indeed know what it is you are doing? And here I would refer the reader to a little work I have written on " The Love of our Lord Jesus Christ," in which I have dwelt upon the duties of a Christian, and have spoken, particularly in one chapter, of the zeal which ought to animate us in preventing the desecration of our churches, and the means we ought to employ for that object. The observation I have just made with regard to irreverences in holy places, I must extend to all other sins. Alas! who has the courage to exert himself as much as he might to put a stop to profane swearing? Oaths and imprecations are to be heard on all sides, indoors and out, and every one goes his way without saying a word. Where is the magistrate who directs his officials to keep on the watch, and note offences of this kind, and make their report to him? Such practice would be most beneficial in many towns, and especially on the wharfs and in thoroughfares, where numbers of porters and others at work there utter the most horrible oaths. Trusty persons might be set to watch and give information quietly and judiciously, and there is no doubt that if some were punished, it would intimidate the others. And after all, is it not most certain that if a conspiracy were formed in these places against the authority of the king, a remedy would speedily be provided? O judges, O magistrates, will you not show as much consideration for a God? Will no one interest himself in His behalf? Our kings have religiously issued proclamations against these disorders, but who will take the trouble to have them put in force? O sir, O madam, your dog is beaten and you resent it; one of your pigeons is killed and you demand justice, you prosecute the offender; but what have you done for your Creator? Truly my spirit and my heart fail within me as I commit to writing this insensibility of the creature towards its Creator, and I stand utterly confounded. But, in fact, the same may be said of all other sins. People think but little of applying a remedy, and the cause of my God is altogether neglected: they blush and are ashamed to take any part in the matter.

But that licentiousness should proceed so far as even to ridicule religion; that people should scoff at those who go often to communion, and give themselves to prayer and other suchlike works, this is what is inconceivable—I do not say, to a truly Christian mind, but to one which retains a vestige of reason. And that I may convince these very scoffers and libertines themselves, I would ask them what there is to ridicule in one who applies himself assiduously to beseech the mercy of God, to pray to Him and adore Him. I would beg them to answer me if this be a subject for laughter and mockery. I would ask them if the greatest honour a creature can have bestowed upon it be not to receive within it the God of al greatness, who gives it His Body and His Blood to nourish it. And if this Sovereign Lord of all is pleased to pay His creature this honour frequently, seeing that such is the object for which He remains on our altars, I would beg them once more to tell me—what to me is incomprehensible—how their minds can find, I will not say motives, but the semblance, the shadow of a motive, for ridicule in practices which fill the angelic hierarchies with admiration, astonishment, and awe. And yet Christians are to be heard freely ridiculing such persons as apply themselves to prayer, frequent the sacraments, and live retired, in order to have leisure to devote themselves more seriously to the work of their salvation. Egregious folly ! though it be the wise and prudent of the world who use such language ; for it cannot be denied that if these worldly-wise people believe in an eternity, a paradise, a hell, a God, it must be the height of folly to laugh at those who serve Him with more fidelity, and at those practices which promote His honour and glory ; it must be the height of folly to scoff at those who, making more account of God than of the creature, and of eternity than time, labour diligently and earnestly to set in order the affairs of their salvation ; it must be the height of folly to ridicule those who take the surest means of saving their souls, and keep aloof from everything that might involve them in everlasting damnation ; who prefer heaven to earth, a life that will never end to one that passes like a shadow, the delights and the glories of Paradise to the seeming goods of time ; who voluntarily forsake a world which they will one day be forced to quit. To these truths I will add still one more, which cannot be disputed, and I say that even though all men were sure of their salvation, nevertheless, seeing that if heaven there are different degrees of glory, as Scripture testifies, it would still be excessive folly to despise those who aspire to the higher graces, according to the counsel of the Holy Spirit, and who labour with His assistance to rank among the first in a glorious eternity. Certainly it would not be difficult to show by a process of induction that in the present world men always aspire to be something more than they are. The lawyer would be glad to be a counsellor; the counsellor a president; the president a chancellor; the private soldier a captain; the captain a general; the general a commander-in-chief; the count or the duke would be delighted to be a prince; the prince a monarch; and thus in all conditions every one is striving after something higher and better. This being so, is it possible that what is transitory should draw away all hearts, and that which is everlasting should make no impression? or that men should ridicule those who, possessing a true faith, earnestly endeavour to win the rewards of eternal glory? Yet this is the aim of devotion, the laughing-stock of libertines.

However, I am not ignorant that it will be objected that it is the failings of the devout that excite the ridicule with which they are assailed. To this I reply that devotion is not the cause of these failings; that they are personal defects, which no doubt are blameable; but why raise a clamour against devotion, which itself condemns them? Can there be a greater piece of injustice? This devout man and that devout woman have their faults, I allow, and so far they are wanting in devotion; why, then, lay the blame on devotion? I would ask these criticisers of the devout if such as have the character of not being devout are perfect? Do they who are ashamed of devotion, or who make a mock of it, lead an innocent life, without committing at least a single mortal sin? Do they bear with good will the afflictions, losses, or humiliations that befal them? Do they suffer injuries with a gentler spirit? Are they more charitable to the unfortunate, kinder to their enemies, or more detached from the world and worldly desires? Have they a more longing desire for eternity? Are they more occupied with God, more given to divine meditation, more zealous in His cause? Let the faults of both be compared, and it will unquestionably appear that they who make profession of devotion have fewer failings than the others, if all things are impartially weighed and considered. I say further, that we cannot withhold from the devout the praise that is their due for their bold profession of serving God, though at the same time they may have many failings. If a person should profess to serve some prince, or great man, and to support his interest everywhere, is not this in itself to pay him honour? And though such a person should not possess all the qualities we might desire to find in him, is therefore the service of the prince to be disparaged under the pretext that those who are in his service do not acquit themselves as they ought? No; let us blame these personal deficiencies, but let us take heed not to extend the censure to their employment, which is the honourable service of a prince. Oh, if men did but know the real nature of the smallest sin, they would give a thousand lives to prevent were it but a single one! I say, then, that the profession of a devout life, however imperfect, is always commendable in this, that it saves from many offences into which the life of others is allowed to run without reflection.

All these thoughts have occurred to me in considering the subject of Jesus hidden in His servants; for truly it is astonishing beyond expression that in the very midst of the Christian world Jesus should remain unknown in those who most belong to Him. I am not so much surprised that His first disciples were regarded as the offscouring of the world, since they who so despised them showed no respect to their Master. But who could have imagined that persons who call themselves His followers, and who acknowledge Him to be God, would behave so ill to those who endeavour to serve Him generously? Happy they whose life is hidden with Christ in God, that they may appear with Him when He manifests His glory. Then will these scoffers and libertines exclaim, " Miserable fools that we were, these are they whom we had sometime in derision and for a parable of reproach; we esteemed their life madness, and behold how they are numbered among the children of God, and their lot is among the saints.* Lo, after having suffered a little, after having been humbled a little, during a life which has vanished away, they enter into glory unspeakable, into a participation of the very joy of God—happiness surpassing all thought! And we, after a few despicable pleasures, a little wretched applause of the world, of which now nothing remains to us, enter upon woes that shall never end, in the company of devils and of the unhappy spirits of the lost!" O Christian soul, how far better to be hidden from the world, and suffer a little with the Adorable Jesus in this present life!

* Wisdom v. 3-5.

A PRAYER TO THE HOLY SPIRIT.

O ADORABLE SPIRIT, O my God, here in Thy divine
presence I acknowledge that I am nothing, and can
do nothing, without Thee; I cannot speak a word or
write a line as a Christian ought, or even form the
slightest good thought, without Thy divine aid. O my
God, establish Thy glory in my nothingness; by the
operation of Thy divine power turn the very vileness
of Thy creature to Thine honour. Come, O Father
of the poor, into the mind and heart of the poorest
and meanest of all Thy creatures on this sacred day,
on which Thou didst so lovingly descend on the
most holy Mother of Jesus, and His first disciples;
give me part in those gifts which Thou didst communicate to them with so much liberality and mercy.
Oh, dislodge from my heart whatever is not of Thee,
that Thou alone mayst fill it, not only with Thy
gifts, but with Thyself. Oh, let me breathe only Thy
pure love, breathe only through Thy pure love, and for
Thy pure love. Henceforth I belong to God alone,
in whom may my whole life be hid with Jesus, with
Mary in Jesus, with the Saints in Jesus. O Spirit of
light and truth, illuminate with Thy clear and powerful beams the hearts of all my brethren who shall
read this little book, that they may know and love
the hidden life of our good Saviour, to whom be
eternal glory, with the Eternal Father and with
Thee. Amen. Amen.

A PRAYER

TO THE MOST HOLY AND EVER IMMACULATE VIRGIN-MOTHER, MOST WORTHY SPOUSE OF THE HOLY SPIRIT.

REMEMBER, O most gracious Virgin, on this day whereon are commemorated the great communications of the Holy Spirit, thy Spouse, with thy most pure and most holy soul, that thou art the sacred channel through which His divinest graces flow. Prostrate at thy blessed feet, where I would live and die, and desiring by the help of my good Saviour there ever to lie, bound by the closest ties of grace, and the strongest bands of pure love, I beseech thee, O my gracious Mistress, in all humility, to let pour into my poor soul those torrents of grace which thy Adorable Spouse so lovingly communicates, through thee, to those who love and serve Him with a generous and faithful zeal. O holy lover of that Heavenly Spouse, obtain for me that I may be zealous with a disinterested zeal for the sole interests of this God of love, yea, Love Itself. Oh, that I may love Him only, love Him constantly. Obtain for me the great gift of serving Him with final perseverance, that, even till I breathe out my last sigh, I may sigh and breathe but for Him alone; that I may be found worthy in His eyes to labour for His glory, to make Him known to men, to make Him loved, to make Him honoured and adored, as is His due, with the Father and the Son for ever and ever. Amen.

PART II.
PRACTICE OF THE HIDDEN LIFE.

CHAPTER I.

THE HIGH ESTEEM WE OUGHT TO HAVE OF THE HIDDEN LIFE.

THE hidden Christian life possesses so many advantages, establishes the soul in so glorious a peace, comprises so many excellences, exalts to so divine a state, that the utmost that can be said of it will never sufficiently express the blessedness, the height, and the glory of a life so holy. The All-Good God having favoured a certain person with a supernatural light, which revealed to him something of the wonderful excellences which this hidden life contains, he remained rapt in the deepest astonishment. Oh, if men knew (he exclaimed) the delights, the riches, the beauties, and the glory of the hidden life, there is nothing they would not do, nothing they would not give up, to embrace it with courage and fidelity. The light which it pleased our most gracious and most merciful God to give to this person was but momentary, and passed like a flash of lightning, and yet it left him so penetrated with the admirable marvels of the hidden life, that the very thought of it transports him out of himself. It is not that memory recalls to him more than a most indistinct vision, but nevertheless the knowledge that has remained to him, though obscure, ravishes his soul with joy. He well remembers that for the space of a brief moment he beheld what transcends all human thought; and that remembrance is sufficient to make him live in a state of continual admiration of the divine excellences of the hidden life. He would fain go and cry through every town and hamlet, "O men, of what are you thinking when you occupy yourselves with creatures, and labour to know them and be known of them, to love them and be loved by them? How long will you be dull of heart, and love lying?" Ah, no, there is but God alone : God alone, God alone, God alone. Let minds and hearts be emptied of everything that they may be filled with His fulness, and that the whole life of all human kind may be entirely hidden with Christ in God. O my Divine Master, draw me after Thee, O my amiable Saviour, ravish, transport, possess my mind and my heart; let creatures exist no longer for me, but do Thou only suffice for my poor soul, as throughout eternity, so also in time. O Jesus, my Jesus, be Thou the Mind of my mind, the Heart of my heart, the Life of my life, the Soul of my soul ; be Thou my only all in all things and for ever. O holy Virgin, to whom Jesus only has ever been the great and only all from the first moment of Thy immaculate conception ; O blessed angels, who ever burned with flames of pure love, the love of God alone, and you especially to whose protection I have been so mercifully committed ; O ye saints, filled with the pure love of Jesus only, let me live no longer but of this pure love ; let my life be wholly hidden in His divine life, by passing happily from this human state to that which is supernatural and superhuman. O hidden life of my Jesus, O Christian life, hidden with

Jesus in God, let me henceforth aspire after nothing but thy glorious possession. O my desires, O my affections, speed, fly, after a life so little esteemed by people of the world, and so precious in the eyes of God and His holy angels. O my soul, henceforth let us be utterly estranged from all that gives consideration in the eyes of men, their knowledge, and their friendship. Ah! how good is it to be annihilated in their mind and in their heart. Disgrace, repulse, contempt, poverty, misery, and dereliction, how precious are you, since you drive us from our place therein! O hidden life, O hidden life, how lovely thou art!

However, if amid the darkness that besets us, I must say something of this hidden life, I cannot but declare that its excellences are truly admirable. We may affirm that it brings Paradise down to earth, or that it makes men angels, causing them to lead a heavenly life here below. These truths are clearly manifested in the hidden life of the solitaries, whose deserts were called " the abode of God," as cities are called " the abodes of men." And verily it would seem that, as in cities it is the manners of creatures, the society, the conversation, and the occupations of creatures that everywhere predominate, and the ordinary employment of men is to see and be seen, so in solitudes life consists in separation from creatures and in the enjoyment of God after an ineffable manner, who reveals Himself to those who seek Him in truth, who communicates Himself in the sweetest ways to those who quit the society of the world for sake of His love, and favours with His divine converse those who for love of Him renounce all intercourse with creatures. O blessed exchange, to give up the society, the knowledge, and the friendship of creatures, and gain instead the converse, the knowledge, and the friendship of God! O ye people of the world, what objects of compassion are you when you pity those who renounce the world to hide themselves in a life of retirement, or who, remaining in the world, are, as it were, annihilated by opprobrium, contempt, and poverty! Weep not for those blessed dead who die in the Lord; weep for yourselves, and let your grief be inconsolable that you are so blinded that you know not your own blindness, that your blindness amounts to madness, and a madness most culpable, most damnable, since it makes you more attached to the creature than the Creator. Oh! if you had to renounce a thousand worlds, yea millions of worlds, for God, this would be nothing, millions of worlds in His presence being as nothing. O ye who take it so ill that your children, your friends, should leave you to bind themselves more closely to the service of God in the cloister, grieve over your own misery, weep for the hardness of your hearts towards God. I declare that it is a matter of unceasing astonishment to me to observe this excessive blindness in Christian people, and sometimes even in such as make profession of a certain devotion. It so clearly shows how rare is a true love of God, when it is question of giving up self-interest, and renouncing the satisfaction of nature and the love of flesh and blood. These poor blind people know nothing of the advantages to be found in abandoning creatures for the sake of the Creator. Is it possible sufficiently to admire the graces and the gifts which He bestows upon all His faithful servants? Yet it must be confessed that He communicates Himself in a manner altogether extraordinary to those whose life is more hidden; so true is it that where there is less of the creature there is more of the Creator. We have but to consider the life of the solitaries, and we shall see that they were in the habit of conversing familiarly with angels, and enjoyed constant communications with the Sovereign Lord of all, who would seem to have kept nothing hidden from them, but to have revealed to them His divinest secrets, poured into their hearts torrents of spiritual delights, imparted to them His holiest graces, and, often, even a certain share of His power ; subjecting to them the irrational animals and even inanimate things, as well as the devils and all hell, whose frequent assaults served only to yield them glorious triumphs, which they achieved with invincible generosity. Alas for us, seated on the banks of the Babylon of the world, we find only a subject of weeping in our banishment from the favours of the holy Sion ! Alas ! communing with God and His angels is rare indeed amongst us, because our conversation and intercourse with creatures are too frequent.

God appears to Jacob, and he beholds Him "face to face," according to the words of Scripture (Gen. xxxii. 30) ; but it is when he has parted from his flocks, his children, and his family, and is left alone in the darkness of the night. The divine word teaches us that Moses was forty days in contemplation, conversing familiarly with the Infinite Majesty of God ; but, to enjoy a happiness so divine, he enters into a cloud with God, and remains hidden in it. If God manifests Himself to the great prophet Elias in so extraordinary a manner, it is only after a retirement of forty days and forty nights. We read in the 16th chapter of Leviticus (v. 17) that no man was to be present in the tabernacle when the high priest entered into the sanctuary. This was a figure of the disposition in which our hearts ought to be to receive the High Priest of our Souls: I mean the disposition we ought properly to have. Creatures must depart out, that God may enter in; His entrance must be hidden from men. This is why it is written (Exod. xl. 32) of the said tabernacle, that after the ark, the candlesticks, and the altar had been put in, it was filled with the glory of the Lord; but this was not until it had been covered with a sacred cloud. Thus it is also written (Lev. xvi. 2) that the Lord said, He would abide in the cloud.

But it is not enough to say that the most precious communications of grace are granted in abundance to the Christian life, it must also be declared that in a most blessed way it elevates the soul to a union with the principle and source of all graces, even to a union with God Himself. One of the greatest servants of God in our age, Father De Condren, said, that it was not sufficient for the Christian to act in all things with a view to Jesus as his end, he must also regard Him as his model, imitate His life and conduct, and, in fine, look upon Him as a tree into which he has been grafted, and with which consequently he has been most intimately united. And does not the Holy Spirit teach us the same when He tells us that we are "partakers of the divine nature"? (2 Pet. i. 4.) But who can say what is involved in this divine union of the soul with the Divinity? If Jesus, who is Truth Itself, had not revealed it to us, who could ever have conceived it? "That they all may be one," said this amiable Saviour, speaking to His Father of His disciples—"that they all may be one, as Thou, Father, in Me, and I in Thee, that they also may be one in Us" (John xvii. 21). O words of exceeding love! O words which all angels and men can never sufficiently admire! O words to ravish all heaven and earth with astonishment and love! O words of infinite consolation! O my God, my God, my poor soul faints at the thought of so admirable a love. O creatures—would that I could make myself heard from one end of the world to the other, and through the whole habitable earth—O creatures, hearken : we are called, on the testimony of a God, to be one with Him. Most sweet it is to repeat words so divine : to be one with God! Yes, the creature, that lump of clay, that vessel of iniquity, that nothing, that sinful nothing, is called to be, by participation, God. O my soul, hast thou well penetrated this truth? Dost thou really know, and dost thou firmly believe, that thou art called to be one with God? Christians, do you indeed believe this? For, if this be so, what have we to fear, united as we are to His Omnipotence? How can we complain of poverty, rejoicing in His riches? How can we complain of our miseries, our sufferings, or humiliations, being united to the God of all blessedness, all joy, all gladness? Truly there is no faith among us. O my God, did we firmly believe this truth—which, however, is indubitable—we should die of love : we should die of transport and delight. O men, O men, and have you still the hardihood to offend so loving a God? Behold a state all divine to which grace calls us! The only obstacle to our enjoyment of it is attachment to creatures ; the great means that conducts us to it is separation from them : and separation from them is never more surely accomplished than by the hidden life. O hidden life, not only, then, dost thou contain incomparable excellencies, not only dost thou make men angels, but thou makest them gods ! Can anything be conceived more exalted and more glorious ?

Again, can anything be conceived more delightful, seeing that perfect joy is an effect of the perfect union of the soul with God ? This is why I would beseech you especially to observe—nay, to call it to mind from time to time and make it the subject of your meditations—that the Son of God, having asked of His Father this inestimable union of love for His disciples, prays that His joy may be perfectly fulfilled in them : as is related by St. John in the 17th chapter of his Gospel. The reason thereof is most plain ; for he that is perfectly united to anything has a perfect participation in its qualities. This being so, I am not surprised that the Adorable Jesus speaks of the joy of His disciples as of a joy that is full ; for it is thus He calls it. It is, indeed, a joy that is full ; for nothing is wanting to it, seeing that it proceeds from the possession of a God. Thus it fills all the capacity of the soul, it leaves no void in the heart, it fully satisfies all desires. God is an infinite good, and we cannot even imagine anything more to be desired. He is the end and the centre of our hearts ; it is in Him, then, and in Him alone, that they can find perfect repose. He is eternal, and He desires to communicate Himself to the soul eternally. Thus the confidence it enjoys is most sweet, since it finds no limits and sees no end to these divine joys.—And here one word to people of the world : O ye people of the world, reflect a little. You wish for happiness, and with this view you pour forth your whole heart on creatures, in whom you will never find it ; and you keep aloof from God, in whose pure love alone you can enjoy it perfectly and for ever.   It is related of a holy man, confined in a gloomy dungeon beneath a tower, loaded with chains and weighed down with all the miseries of this present life, and that for many years, that at the end he was found filled with unspeakable joy and peace: the reason being that he was united to God alone by pure love. Yes, this union fills the soul with indescribable joy, at least as regards its superior part; for the inferior part is notwithstanding sometimes in an abyss of suffering, as is clearly seen in our Lord; and this joy subsists in the midst of everything that is most frightful and most abhorrent to nature.   But without this union, though you should enjoy all the pleasures, all the possessions, all the honours which the world contains, your desires would never be satisfied, nor your heart fully contented.

But that which ought to inspire us with the highest esteem for the hidden life is the glory which accrues therefrom to God; for, indeed, to one who has ever so little knowledge of God, nothing is of so much importance as His sacred interests.   The hidden life glorifies God in an incomparable manner; for, if the glory of God consists in clear and exalted knowledge of what He is, a knowledge full of love and abounding in praise, assuredly great glory results to His Infinite Majesty from hidden souls; seeing that, flying from the sight of creatures, and denying themselves their esteem and friendship, they rest satisfied with the sight of God only, and with His love alone: and inasmuch as God only is all in all to these souls, they manifest before angels and men that there is nothing like unto Him.   They loudly testify to His perfections; they declare the nothingness of every created being, and, consequently, the unprofitableness, the vanity, and the folly of those who occupy themselves therewith and are attached thereto. They read an admirable lesson to men on these two great truths: viz., that God is the Great All, and that everything which is not God is nothing in His presence. Their separation from creatures clearly marks the knowledge they possess of the Creator. They discover Him to be so infinitely great, that they no longer behold anything out of Him; and as they know but Him only, so also do they love nothing save Him alone. Yes, God alone is their Great, their Only All in all. He is all their honour, all their good, all their pleasure; He is their knowledge, their esteem, their love; He is their treasure, their glory, their recreation, their joy, their life; He is their kindred, their credit, their support, their fortune, all their ambition, all they desire, all they seek after, all they wish for. Truly is not this to render to the Divinity a marvellous testimony of what He is? Is not this to be filled with the most exalted knowledge of Him? Is it not to chant in His honour a new song of matchless praise, and of a love most pure and all divine?

If, then, I am asked of what use are hidden souls—what glory God derives from them—what good they do to those about them and to the world at large—it it is easy for me to reply that the glory they render to God is unspeakable, and that the whole world is benefited by them to a degree which words cannot express. We have briefly stated what they are with reference to God, and the little that has been said, if understood in some slight measure, clearly teaches that hidden souls glorify God in an incomparable manner. And in truth—to descant a little more on a subject so vast, and one that can never be exhausted by man—although it is most certain that the active and public life of faith is the great means by which the glory of God is promoted—so that one of the early Fathers of the Church called it the most divine of all divine things—when it is employed for the conversion of sinners, the sanctification of the just, the declaration of the mysteries and the perfections of God, yet it must be confessed that the admixture of corrupt nature, the self-satisfaction, the self-interest, which are so often to be found therein, are hindrances to the glory of God, so that it subtracts from it on the one hand, while it furthers it on the other. Men say and preach that God only is to be esteemed and loved: this it is which directors inculcate, this it is which preachers enforce, this it is which persons who live in the world and have a zeal for God are ever protesting, and therein they glorify His Most Adorable Majesty and uphold His divine interests. But the misfortune is this—that after having duly said and preached that God only is to be esteemed and loved, they deny in their actions what they have maintained in their words. Directors, preachers, and others engaged in exterior works, so far from being satisfied with God alone, seek the esteem and friendship of creatures, and are glad to have their approbation and to possess a place in their mind and heart: their natural feelings and self-love betray themselves in their intercourse with others, in their conversations, and in their friendships. Sometimes it is only some slight gratification of nature, very trifling and scarcely perceptible, but nevertheless it is a gratification of nature. Alas! where will you find amid exterior occupations a mind, a heart, wholly detached from creatures and content with God alone ?   This sad truth becomes too apparent in the gentle complaints you hear them make, the pain they seem to suffer, when their penitents or their hearers treat them unkindly ; when they do not succeed in the good works they undertake ; when they are found fault with, not only by people of the world, but by devout persons ; when they meet with slight and repulse, or are defamed and calumniated : for if they desired but God alone, what reason have they to be troubled, seeing that He still remains to us, and that more purely ?   Surely it is because along with God they wish to possess the creature, and the creature is easily to be found—yes, I repeat it, easily to be found—in exterior occupations. I say, further, that unless we watch ourselves most strictly by means of continued mortification, aided by the most powerful graces, self-love finds wherewith to féast and pamper itself after the most delicate fashion in such works as have our neighbours for their object. Daily experience teaches us that creatures in a state of corruption have a strange power of infecting and spoiling one another.   It was a good saying, then, of him who declared that as often as he associated with men he returned less a man.   We become attached to one another, if not after the common and vulgar manner, yet in a refined and subtle way ; natural feelings come to mix themselves with these attachments ; self-love finds its own account in pious meetings, in direction, and in preaching ; and this happens very frequently when there are numbers seeking our direction, attending our preaching, or coming to confer with us ; neither are employments among less cultivated people exempt from these snares.   Wherever the creature is, there is room for attachments.

Now it is here that we may perceive the advantages of the hidden life : a life hidden, whether by being separated from the sight and knowledge of creatures, or by being annihilated in their mind and heart by poverty, contempt, and opprobrium. One who knows and who is known of creatures, who is loved, admired, sought after, and esteemed by them, may, indeed, say God Only, and may say it in truth ; but how hard and how rare a thing this is ! How often does that God Only of whom he speaks behold something other than Himself in his mind and in his heart ! Ah ! how often is there some admixture of the creature ! A great servant of God in our times, the late M. De Renty, used to say that he was convinced that the greater proportion of our evils proceeds from our taking pleasure in seeing and being seen ; that this dangerous amusement conceals a venom most detrimental to the progress of the soul, although it does not perceive the injury or feel the wound ; that what sullies the purity of acts of piety is that self-love desires to have them known and observed ; that we always exhibit ourselves in the best light, and hide our defects and the reverse of the picture ; that our whole exterior is so studied, that our interior is often more occupied therewith than with God ; and that there are few persons who do not care about the vain regard of creatures either in a passive or in an active way. This is not the case in the hidden life : they who really lead this life say God Only, and say it truly ; their actions bear faithful witness to their words. They truly seek the notice, the esteem, and the friendship of God Only, since they have no desire to be seen, esteemed, or loved by any living creature whatsoever ; this is why they are transported and exult with joy when they are unknown and unthought of: or if, in the order of Divine Providence, they are obliged to live and converse with creatures, they remain hidden amongst them through the annihilations which they suffer by being deserted, despised, and spoken against. Ah! then it is that, thrust aside by men, effaced from their memory, banished from their heart, they cry out with truth that God Only is their all in all. They say it, and God sees it. Then it is that they render Him a glory great beyond all comparison: for, stripping themselves of everything but Him, remembering nothing but Him, they render to His Divinity the highest and the strongest testimony of gratitude and love which they can pay Him, being ready also to sacrifice to Him their life itself. Souls which allow any admixture of the love and esteem of created things are thereby far removed from such pure love and zeal for His glory: for after all, let us employ ourselves as much as we will in directing, preaching, making conversions, visiting the hospitals, assisting the unfortunate, yet if, along with our love of God and zeal for His glory, there be any admixture of self-love—I acknowledge, indeed, that God is glorified by all these actions, but—I say that at the same time His glory suffers by this admixture, inasmuch as it prevents God being all in all to the soul, and evidences in a manner its weakness, and a defect in the knowledge it has of Him, as well as in the praise and love it renders to Him. For I pray you to consider that, whatever good works a man may do, if God is not all-sufficient to him, he does not glorify Him perfectly, seeing he is not contented with an Infinite Being. Shall not God, who is sufficient to Himself, be sufficient for man? Is it truly to know

Him, is it fitly to praise Him, and, consequently, is it worthily to glorify Him, not to be satisfied with Him alone?   Is it not true that the heart of one who does so many good deeds, and yet is not entirely free from all admixture of the creature, is but imperfectly subject to the dominion of its sovereign?   Jesus lives therein by His grace, He works great things therein by His power; but He does not reign therein absolutely, since everything displeasing to Him is not removed.   Thus He does not effect all He would do; His divine will is not thoroughly accomplished. But He reigns sovereignly in the soul of one who leads a hidden life, who, making no reservation of his own wishes, at least with full consciousness, apart from the will of God, desires only what He desires, and desires Him alone in all things.   Such a one performs external acts when God requires it of him, but without leaving His sole beloved All, abiding ever hidden with Jesus in God alone, and seeking no share in creatures.   The divine solitude wherein he dwells keeps him so far aloof from the esteem and love of the world, and from all that the world loves, that it seems to have no existence for him.   In saying all this, we must be understood to mean nothing but what is in accordance with the orthodox doctrine of the Church, Catholic, Apostolic, and Roman, which declares that, except by special privilege, the holiest souls do still fall into venial faults in this life; but certainly this happens to them only by surprise, and never with their full and entire advertence; and, as St. Jerome says, the failings of saints might at times very well pass for perfections in others.   In fine, God takes His delight in such souls as perfectly satisfy Him, inasmuch as they are satisfied with Him only, which He does not in others, whatever they may do in His service. And here it must be observed that the good pleasure of God consists, and is fulfilled, in the accomplishment of what He desires of us: in doing much, if He so ordains; in doing nothing, if such be His will. But whether we do much, or whether we do nothing, every way we must desire but Him alone: for from the moment we desire anything else but Him, we do not fully satisfy Him. This brings to the test those persons who pour themselves forth on external things; for if they distress themselves when, in the order of Divine Providence, they can no longer pursue their labours, either through infirmity, or because their services are no longer required, it is a sign that along with God they have desired something else. Oh, how true it is, that there are few who are contented to find nothing in creatures, and to whom God alone suffices!

But when God finds souls thus pure, disinterested, and faithful, He gives Himself to them with such profuse outpourings of His divinest graces, that He seems to have nothing in reserve for them. Nevertheless, after He has bestowed His most precious graces, He gives Himself to them with yet further excesses of love unspeakable. If it is written (Psalm cxliv. 19) that He will fulfil all the desire of them that fear Him; how much more of those who belong to Him alone through His only and most pure love! These are the souls that obtain from Him the sweetest favours and that impetrate the greatest mercies. These are they that sustain the weight of His wrath, that turn away His anger from the people, and stay His chastising hand. We must not, then, think that such souls are useless to mankind, seeing that it is by them the world is upheld, that kingdoms, provinces, and cities are preserved. The world long ago deserved to be destroyed by its crimes; the sins of men long since deserved the most terrible chastisements of the avenging justice of God. If the world still subsists, if we do not experience the terrible effects of the anger of God, it is owing only to the multitude of His great mercies. But these great mercies are granted for the sake of those souls which God so lovingly regards, because they look to Him alone, that there is nothing He would not do for love of them. These souls, so precious in His sight, disarm His vengeance when He is about to hurl His thunders on our guilty heads. When He is preparing to let fall His scourges on some city, province, or kingdom, a few such souls have power to avert His wrath. And what do they not effect in the order of grace! Be assured of this, that often, in the sight of God, to them is due the glory of the great marvels which He works in the justification and sanctification of souls, although externally He uses for His purposes preachers, missionaries, and directors. The reason is this :—It is most true that the numerous and extraordinary conversions of sinners, heretics, and unbelievers, as well as the exalted sanctification of chosen souls, are triumphs of a special grace. It is most true that preachers and directors are the instruments by which these things are wrought; that they are the channels through which flow those precious and divine graces. It is also most true that without these graces all their talents, all their eloquence, all their reasonings, would prove unavailing. But when God bestows His graces for the sake of hidden souls, as He very frequently does, is it not true that the persons and countries thus converted owe to these souls, after God, the greatest obligation? The people of Israel fought valiantly against powerful enemies, and achieved a glorious victory; but Scripture teaches us that the glory was due to the prayers of Moses. Certainly one who looked no further than the mere exterior would have no manner of doubt that the triumph of the Israelites was due to their own valour and warlike strength. True it is that God made use of their arms and their valour; but, after all, it was to the prayers of one of His servants, Moses alone, that He granted the victory, and without the prayers of this man of God, both the arms and the valour of the people of God would have been without avail. Let preachers and directors reflect seriously on this truth, drawn from the divine word; let others consider it attentively, and let all learn that sometimes a single person, wholly hidden from the eyes of men, obtains abundantly from God all those largest graces which He communicates through direction, missions, and preaching. We have an illustrious instance of this in the "Life of Sister Marie de Valence," which was published some years ago, and which underwent a careful examination at the hands of many doctors of theology at Paris, by command of the late Queen-Mother, whose simple faith and exemplary piety will be blessed for ages to come. Now this life, which was approved after strict examination, relates that our Lord revealed to this soul, so singularly favoured by God, and so highly praised by St. Francis of Sales, Cardinal Richelieu, Father Cotton of the Company of Jesus, and other eminent personages, who all knew her—her life, I say, tells us that our Lord revealed to her that for her sake He would convert a very great number of sinners and unbelievers, and would even raise many souls to the most exalted ways of perfection; indeed, the number mentioned is astonishing. In order thoroughly to understand this truth, we have only to consider the Most Blessed Virgin, who, retired apart in her humble abode, neither preached nor administered any sacrament, and yet it cannot be doubted but that she was more useful to the world than apostolic men and all other persons who were most actively employed in external works. "Doubtless," said St. Teresa, "a soul in perfect union with God, although it leads a retired life, does not go to heaven unaccompanied; it takes thither a great number of souls by its prayers." The same must be said of those who, although bound by their state to hear confessions, preach, and direct, are prevented from discharging these duties by the opposition they encounter. Alas! they who look only at the outside of things imagine they remain useless in the midst of their abasement; but they know not that by serving as victims to the divine justice for sinners, for the cities, dioceses, and provinces in which they suffer, they appease His wrath, and obtain incalculable benefits and unspeakable blessings for those places where they have thus been trodden under foot, whilst the glory is given to those who have laboured externally to procure them. And it is a fact very worthy of remark that there are certain souls whom God is so desirous of hiding from the eyes of men, that while He accomplishes great things by their means, it is His will that this should remain entirely unperceived. For instance, He will be pleased to restore health to some sick person by their means, to bestow justifying grace on some sinner, to show some great mercy to a city or a state; He will cause them to pray for all these things with groanings unutterable; He will make them suffer, and there shall be none but themselves who know it; nay, sometimes they themselves shall not be aware of the effect of their prayers and sufferings. Blessed souls! wholly reserved for God alone, of whom He is so divinely jealous that he takes from them every occasion of attachment either to creatures or to themselves, preventing at the same time others from becoming attached to them through the esteem in which they would hold them if they knew their merits, or the blessings and graces which God bestows for their sakes. O precious state, all holy, all divine, and yet, alas! this is the state which all the world flies from, from which even the devout turn away, corrupt nature not enduring to be deprived of the knowledge, the esteem, and the friendship of creatures. Hence arises a secret inclination to speak of the graces we have received, of our own interior, and of the good it is in our power to do. Let us repeat it: there are few souls to whom God alone suffices.

All these considerations appear to me amply sufficient to convince men of the greatness of the hidden life; but, over and above all these, there is one thing which seems to afford irresistible proof of its excellencies; and that is the esteem and love which a God-made-man evinced for this life. O the depth of the riches of the wisdom and of the knowledge of God! how incomprehensible are His judgments! How true is it that His holiest and divinest ways look like simple folly to the wise and prudent of this world, the philosophers of the age! Say to these wise and prudent men according to the flesh, that the Sovereign Lord of all, the Creator of the world, became man, and for thirty years of His life remained hidden in the work-shop of a poor artisan, Himself exercising the trade of a carpenter—these truths find no entrance into their minds; and assuredly such conduct is beyond the reach of the merely human mind. For who would have ex-pected that, if a God became man, and lived and con-versed visibly with men for four-and-thirty years, He would pass thirty of them hidden in the obscure work-shop of a carpenter? Could the mind of man, unless it yielded itself to the teachings of grace, conceive that such would be the employment and occupation of a God? A God becomes man, and of the thirty-four years He has resolved to spend on our earth, He employs thirty in abiding hidden in the house of a poor carpenter: this is beyond our comprehension, and yet it is this that marks the very great predilec-tion of this God-Man for the hidden life, and that gives us cause to exclaim, with the devout Thomas à Kempis, in one of his works, "Verily, there is something very great in the hidden life, seeing that the Adorable Jesus loved it so ardently." The predilec-tion and love that a God-Man showed for it is a stronger reason in its favour than all that men and angels could adduce: what, then, if my mind be unenlightened on the subject? what if I be unable to understand and comprehend anything of it? sufficient for me that I know the esteem which my God enter-tained for the hidden life, to have the highest con-viction of its greatness. All the lights which men possess are limited, and subject to imperfection; my God possesses lights that are infinite, and a goodness that has no bounds; so that He can neither deceive nor be deceived. And further we may say, that what is most apparent and most remarkable in the life of this

God-Man during the three or four years He conversed with men, is not what is most divine therein.   The great and wonderful things that passed in His interior, known and seen only by His Eternal Father, unknown and hidden from the eyes of creatures, exceed all thought, and leave us, filled with admiration and astonishment, to adore them in reverential silence : so true is it that He remains ever a hidden God, even when He manifests himself the most.   The thought also occurs, that those creatures who are exalted to the highest glory, are they whose life was least known to men ; and very meet it is that the members which are most closely united to such a Head, and which have the deepest sympathy with Him, should have the largest share in a life which formed His sweetest delight on earth.   Thus, if I cast my eyes on the most holy Virgin, St. Joseph, and St. John Baptist—of whom the Scripture tells us (John x. 41) that he wrought no miracle, and passed almost all his life in the desert, and at last ended it in the gloomy darkness of a prison, perishing ignominiously by the hand of an executioner,—I see before me the most glorious inhabitants of Paradise, who shall stand at the head of all the blessed for all eternity.   O my brother, O my sister, whoever you are, rejoice if you are unknown to the world, if your existence is scarcely recognized ; or, if you are known to the world, that it is only to be crucified, and to be made a by-word and a reproach.   It is true you are not called to lead the life or perform the office of Apostles ; you are neither preachers nor directors ; and it seems as if you were useless on this earth of ours ; but, seeing that you can love God purely and faithfully, according to His commandments, your

condition is so much the more to be prized as it has
more resemblance to that of the Mother of God, St.
Joseph, and St. John Baptist.   And if this be so, can
you complain of a state so blessed?

CHAPTER II.

WE OUGHT TO GIVE OUR AFFECTIONS TO THE HIDDEN LIFE WITH COURAGE AND FIDELITY.

WE may love the hidden life in many different ways.
Some are called to it by withdrawal into a perfect external solitude, like the holy Fathers of the Desert;
others are drawn to it by vocation to a religious life of
great retirement, like the Carthusians, Benedictines,
and certain private individuals.   There are some who,
through the grace of our Lord, are led to embrace it,
although they live in the world, by discreetly avoiding all unnecessary visits and conversation, and
remaining in solitude as much as they are able.
There are others who live hidden, although their
state of life obliges them to appear in public, by fore-
going in a Christian spirit all intercourse with the
great, and shunning the acquaintance of persons of
distinction, never willingly coming forward, or seeking the esteem and friendship of any creature, keeping
their graces secret, and preserving a profound silence
on all things, without exception, which could attract
to themselves the esteem of men.   Finally, there are

others whom Divine Providence conceals by their low extraction, their intellectual inferiority, their deficiency in natural talents, their poverty, the contempt in which they are held, the slights that are put upon them, the little success they meet with in their employments, the loss of reputation, the desertion of all they hold most dear, and the calumnies raised against them.   The duty of each in these several conditions is to abide with love and fidelity in that state in which the order of Divine Providence has placed him.

But most certain it is that the love of the hidden life is essential to us in whatever state we are, in so far as it leads us to content ourselves with God alone, and in no way to seek the esteem or friendship of creatures.   Let us live as solitaries, if the All-Good God so requires of us: it is of such that the holy book of " The Imitation of Christ " has said that it is a praiseworthy thing to avoid the sight of men. Oh, how holy, how divine, are monastic institutions, which, by securing a complete seclusion from creatures, raise souls to the purest union with the Creator !

Oh, what graces and benedictions are theirs who by their zeal, strict discipline, and good life shall always maintain the exact performance of their holy rule ! But woe, a terrible woe, to those who by their tepidity, weak indulgence, human respect, and desire of their own comfort, shall introduce therein the least relaxation !

It is certain that we cannot err in discreetly avoiding creatures.   I say *discreetly*, that we may not do anything contrary to the vocation of our state; speaking and conversing, when necessary, in the order of God's appointment, and where His glory is concerned. What we must be mindful of is never to put ourselves forward at the suggestion of natural inclination, but to abandon ourselves simply to the Spirit of Jesus Christ, that we may be solely what He would have us to be, and be nothing at all when His loving Providence shall so dispose.

If we love God purely, assuredly He will suffice us. Ah! how easy it will then be to us to dispense with creatures, how sweet will it be to be separated from them. And, truly, to that soul to which God alone suffices, company and conversation are irksome : it finds its dearest delight in solitude and retirement, it neither sees, nor is seen, save by the eyes of divine charity. Those persons who can scarcely endure retirement, who seek the society of creatures, give evident proofs how little they converse with God.

If, however, Divine Providence call us to a life of intercourse with the world, let us take care not to throw ourselves into it unreservedly, or pour forth our minds upon it by needless and superfluous attention. It is a striking fact which is related of St. Mary Magdalene of Pazzi, that she knew by divine revelation that when she went to speak to persons who came to see her, she usually committed faults on those occasions, and returned from such conversations with some diminution of her perfection ; and yet this great saint breathed only God, spoke only of God, and inflamed with the fires of divine love all who approached her. Wonderful, but terrible example, to those religious who love the parlour, or who find ready excuses to frequent it.

If we are obliged to hold conversation, let us confine ourselves to what is necessary ; and above all, when the persons with whom we converse are of a different sex to ourselves, let us adhere most strictly to this rule.

That servant of God of whom it is related that he never sat down when conversing with women, in order to avoid all useless words, can never be sufficiently commended, and his memory ought to be precious to all those souls who desire only the glory of God alone. So far as depends upon ourselves let us fly from creatures, let us sigh after retirement, let us take delight in being solitary.

So far as rests with ourselves, let us sincerely desire that our very existence be unknown to men. But if we are known in the world, let us be known in it for Jesus Christ our Master's sake. Away with the prudence and the wisdom of this world, which under specious pretexts lead us to obtrude ourselves on its notice. Let us not willingly associate with the great, or mix with what is called "the world," which has this property belonging to it, that it removes us as far from God as it brings us nigh to creatures.

Ah ! how many, I will not say seculars, but ecclesiastics, and even religious of the strictest rule, have lost their first fervour of spirit, and have fallen into a state of most dangerous tepidity, through having been admitted to intercourse with the great people of the world !

Every one may think what he pleases, but I know that the saints, moved in a special manner by the Holy Spirit, have ever had great fear of being brought into contact with worldly society. We may with truth say that the atmosphere of the world is infectious, that it is like an atmosphere tainted with pestilence.

It is difficult, it is most unusual, for persons to remain in it for any time without contracting the infection of so dangerous a malady. We may even go further, and say that let the time be ever so short during which we remain within its influence —nay, should we but allow our thoughts to dwell upon it—we expose ourselves to the evident danger of death.

O my Lord and my God, lay open before men the infection and the poison of what is called " fashionable life."

O my God, how melancholy to see those who were so separate from creatures and the world, such lovers of poverty and contempt, so strangely transformed by association with the gay world that they seem altogether different people from what they were, both by their declension from the high standard of Christian morality and by their change of life.

We must observe that persons do not go all lengths at once. At first they stand firm, they are full of great designs for the glory of God alone, they sigh over the maxims and the life of those with whom they associate, they address them earnestly on the holiness of the maxims of Jesus Christ, they declaim against the wickedness of the world, and the All-Merciful God even bestows a blessing on what they say ; but, without a very special grace and extraordinary watchfulness, little by little they accustom themselves to the world's ways. They relax something either in their manner of living or in their dress, or in their conversation, under the plea of accommodating themselves to others with the best intentions, so as not to give offence, and thereby be more useful.

Their conscience grows easy, they become very human-very complaisant ; they speak little of God, they talk like philosophers, like the wise and prudent of this world ; they spend a large portion of their time in paying and receiving visits ; the spirit of prayer grows weaker in them, if ever they possessed it ; insensibly they begin to set a value on this world's greatness, they lose the taste for poverty and contempt, and become at last worldly with the worldly, although in a rather more refined way ; they grow self-interested, fond of their own ease, jealous of their own honour ; they become immersed in the world's affairs and busied with its news, and have no longer any time to give to meditation and the contemplation of the great and awful truths of eternity. They suit themselves to everybody's humour, they seek to make themselves agreeable to persons of distinction, and avoid the society of those servants of God who live unnoticed.

Penetrated with a sense of these dangers, the late Father John Chrysostom, a religious penitent of the third order of St. Francis, could not be persuaded to go and dine every week with a person of rank, although that person was leading a most exemplary life, and sought his society only that he might become more inflamed with the love of God ; although he offered to bestow considerable alms upon his house, and contribute largely towards the expense of building a convent of his Order ; and although he was a man of great prudence and held important offices. This man of God preferred depriving himself of the abundant aids he might have received for his Order, to exposing himself to the dangers abounding in the great world, even among persons of piety.

The late Father Bagot of the Company of Jesus,

one of the most learned men of our time, but even far more learned in the science of the saints than in that of the schools, held it for an axiom that frequent intercourse with the great world was very dangerous. And since, in the Providence of God, I have been led to make mention of one of His eminent and faithful servants, I will here relate three remarkable traits of this great man.

The first is that, having a natural inclination for study, and being, as I have said, a man of great acquirements, nevertheless, at the time that he was engaged in preparing his works for publication, he would at once quit his studies and his literary labours for the youngest scholar in the college who might ask for him, and spend considerable time in conversing with him; and when some one spoke to him with admiration of his conduct, he answered, " When I study, I endeavour to do it in the order of God's Providence, and for God; when I converse with a young scholar, I consider that I do it in the same order, and thus it is a matter of complete indifference to me." O man, truly dead to man, who no longer acts by the spirit of man, but by the Spirit of Jesus Christ !

The second thing which appears to me very remarkable is that he could never endure any sort of praise of himself, while at the same time he treated others with marked respect, and willingly bestowed commendation upon them. I know that one day he inveighed with holy anger against one of his friends, because he had learned that on some occasion he had spoken advantageously of him. Rare example, but one which it would be well to imitate.

The third is his admirable patience, which he

especially displayed when, having arrived at an advanced age, he underwent an operation for the stone, from which he suffered greatly.

And here I cannot but magnify the compassion of Jesus and Mary towards those who are devout to them. This good servant of the Son and of the Mother had so great a fear of this disorder that when he was quite a youth he was ready to faint at the very thought of it; and yet, notwithstanding his great age and infirmity, he endured the operation with such Christian fortitude as even to encourage the surgeons who were performing it, although it lasted a more than usual length of time; and while no complaint escaped his lips, he was heard only to say, "I fill up those things that are wanting of the sufferings of Christ" (Col. i. 24). I know not if it were his ardent desire for death which inspired him with such great tranquillity at times when his life was in jeopardy, but I know well that in another dangerous disorder his joy was so great at the thought that he should not recover, that the physicians considered it had much contributed to the restoration of his health. This occasioned him lively sorrow, as I myself was made aware when, on having afterwards the happiness of seeing him, he begged me to console him for not having died. He expired shortly after in a state of wonderful, or, rather, divine peace, although his end was sudden, a few hours only of the night being allowed him for preparing himself, if we may so speak of one who was every moment desiring the dissolution of His body, that he might be with Jesus and Mary. We may believe that the all-merciful God poured His benedictions abundantly on this holy man on account of his faith, which was so eminent and so pure; as also for the veneration with which he regarded the Sovereign Pontiff, a veneration most profound and worthy of a truly Catholic soul; and, again, to reward his humility, which was so great that he took counsel of persons beneath him, for instance, the very students, on occasions following their opinions, adopting their suggestions, and acting on their advice; and lastly, because of his singular devotion to the Mother of God, that sacred channel through which the God of all goodness makes to flow in abundance His sweetest and purest graces. I may say also that God sent to him souls of singular excellence, that he might be their director in the highest ways of perfection. Among many others may be mentioned Father Jogues, of the Company of Jesus, whose memory is blessed for his holy life and precious death, God having bestowed upon him the glory of dying, whilst he was preaching the gospel in Canada, amidst all the tortures that the cruelty of barbarians could invent. Father Mélau of the same Company was also one of the spiritual children of this man of God. He died at Bernay, a town of Normandy, while passing through on his way to Rouen, leaving behind among men so high an opinion of his sanctity, that the people, as by a secret inspiration, feel themselves moved to seek his aid in their wants and necessities. It is sufficient to say of him that he made that great vow of performing all his actions to the greater glory of God, without mentioning the extraordinary graces and favours which were bestowed upon him; and he had also under his direction the first illustrious bishops of China, Cochin China, Tonquin, and Canada. He called them his joy and his crown; and, in truth, it was by his counsel and guidance, of which the Spirit of God made use, that these evangelical missions were established, which without exaggeration may be reckoned amongst the most important and most celebrated in the Church.

But to return to our subject: we will say that if we are obliged to converse with creatures, we ought at least never to seek their friendship or approbation; being well pleased to have no share in their mind or in their heart, and thus remaining hidden. Let us, then, rejoice in all the means with which Divine Providence supplies us for being little thought of in the world, even when we mix in it; as, for instance, low birth, deficiency in natural talents, want of position, or engagement in humble and mean occupations, failure in our undertakings, the little esteem entertained for us, the neglect into which we fall, the exposure of our faults, or the calumnies raised against us.

Certainly it is enough to make us die of shame when we reflect upon our disinclination for a life which was the object of the sweetest complacency and tenderest affection of the saints. The saints loved it supremely—witness St. Onufrius, who passed sixty years of his life in the desert,—or St. Paul the Hermit, who there abode in perfect solitude—leading a life more angelic than human, a life belonging rather to heaven than to earth, for they beheld but God alone, loved but God alone, and God alone sufficed them in all things; and this is the life of the blessed, to which we aspire. This is why the inclinations of the souls that are most dear to God, lead them to the life hidden with Christ in God alone. The Venerable Mary Magdalen of St. Joseph, a Carmelite nun of the great convent of Paris, a soul singularly honoured by our gracious

Saviour, the Blessed Virgin, the angels, and the saints, and rendered famous by the miracles that happened after her precious death, had desired to live while on earth among shepherds and obscure persons ; this, however, being out of her power, she asked permission to be a lay sister, but being unable to obtain her desire, she neglected nothing by which she might pass a life of concealment in a house which was honoured by visits from the highest personages in the realm, including the queen and the princesses. And, in fact, she continued for twenty years this obscure mode of life, deputing her sub-prioress to entertain the queen so long as she was superioress, and even threatening one of the religious that she would give up directing her if she talked of her to the queen, Marie de Medicis, who at that time was in the habit of going once a week to the Convent of the Incarnation in the Faubourg St. Jacques. The souls dearest to God have loved the hidden life even to tenderness. They experienced an incomparable joy whenever they could withdraw from the sight of creatures ; retirement formed their sweetest delight ; it was one of their innocent pleasures to invent all sorts of devices for leading a hidden life, and sometimes they even had recourse to holy artifices to conceal from others what they really were, either by a complete flight, retiring into unfrequented places, going into countries where their character and virtues were necessarily unknown, or by their disclosure of faults which they had formerly committed ; or, again, by drawing attention to their natural defects, and to such things as in the estimation of the world are matter of some confusion ; or by the simplicity of their words and conversation, their poor and mean attire, and manner of living. It is related of the great St. Martin that his dress was rough and coarse, and that he entirely neglected his outward appearance; and, as he travelled in this condition, he ordered the ecclesiastics who accompanied him to walk some distance before or behind him, that he might not be recognized by those who met him. This plan succeeded so perfectly according to his wishes that (as has been before said) he was sometimes exceedingly ill-treated by disorderly persons who did not know him by sight, though his name was celebrated throughout the world. Father John Chrysostom (of whom we have before spoken) had such a tender affection for the hidden life, that he was often heard expressing his longing desire for anything that could conduce thereto. "Let us go," he used to say, "let us go and say Mass in the least frequented churches; let us go and hide ourselves;" and this is what he would say when performing some journey of devotion in the company of other persons of piety. It is also known that it had been his design to retire into a desert could he have obtained permission. Saints have preferred the hidden life to all the distinctions, all the honours, all the pleasures, all the goods, and all the glory of the world; many great princes and princesses having voluntarily abdicated their kingdoms and all their grandeur, to go and bury themselves alive in the obscurity of retirement. Saints have loved the hidden life even, as it might seem, to excess: witness St. Ignatius, the founder of the Company of Jesus, who in his capacity of superior commanded his confessor, Father Eguia, to take the discipline, and laid upon him a severe penance, because he inadvertently said something in his praise; and it has even been believed that this great saint by his prayers obtained that this good father should die a short time before his own death, that he might be prevented publishing abroad the great and admirable virtues, the marvellous, the truly divine fervour, which had been bestowed upon him by heaven, and of which this father had cognizance in his office of confessor.*   Saints

* The account given in the "Life of St. Ignatius" is as follows: "There was nothing which so shocked and disturbed his humility as the reputation of sanctity. Having understood that a brother of the house had said to another that Ignatius was a great saint, he sent for him, and, after reproving him sharply for doing such dishonour to sanctity as to recognize it in a sinner like him, he said that it was a blasphemy, and condemned him to eat his meals for two weeks in the foulest place in the house. For a like indiscretion, Father Diego d'Eguia, after rigid penance, had the term of his life abridged. Being a holy man and his confessor, Ignatius revealed to him certain graces which God had conferred upon his soul, commanding him to reveal them to none. But Diego, full of astonishment, and not able to speak or yet be silent, broke out into certain exclamations, as that Ignatius was a saint, and more than a saint, with like expressions, which he uttered in simplicity, but which some who heard were offended by. On hearing of it, Ignatius took another confessor, and imposed on him (Diego) that he should give himself a public discipline on three evenings in succession, and recite three Psalms in which mention is made of restraining the tongue and not giving scandal to others. Still the good old man could not refrain from saying words which, though they seemed allowable to him, were still a breach of what was imposed upon him. He said that he hoped he might outlive Ignatius, if it were only a few hours, so that he might be released from this command, and be able to speak, and tell such strange things that the world would be astonished. It is related by Olivier Manareo, and was the belief of all the fathers who then lived, that this prayer caused the saint to make another prayer, and that, for the comfort of his own humility, he besought God that the death of Eguia might precede his own, which it did by a few days. So did he shrink from the reputation of sanctity, that he could not endure that it should follow after his death; and for the same reason he prayed God not to illustrate him by miracles."

Oratorian Life, vol. ii. pp. 143, 144.

have loved the hidden life even to holy folly. How many of them have performed ridiculous actions, like St. Francis of Assisi and his first companions! The history of the early Jesuits furnishes also admirable examples of this, and especially the life of that most holy man, Father Balthazar Alvarez. Every one knows what was done by the Blessed John of God. And St. Simeon Salus was so divinely enamoured of the hidden life, that the ardour of his love made him spend his days in a succession of seeming extravagances, even to the very moment of his death. Saints have loved the hidden life even so far as to wish to be possessed bodily by the devil rather than that their real selves should be known ; and this it is that is narrated of this saint ; for having the gift of miracles and, in particular, that of casting out devils, in order that men might cease to entertain for him the high esteem with which they regarded him, he begged of God that he might be himself possessed, as really happened to him a little before his death. This example is more to be admired than imitated, but it strongly marks the predilection of the saints for the hidden life. Saints have so loved it as to prefer death itself to the loss of it. Such we read to have been the sentiments of that holy Solitary who, perceiving that men wished to make him a bishop in spite of himself, obtained from God the favour of dying before he could be withdrawn from his beloved retreat. Saints have loved the hidden life, not only during life and at the hour of death, but even after death. Father De Condren, when he was dying, begged he might be buried deep in the ground somewhere on the outside of Paris, in order that his tomb might not be a means of preserving his memory. It pleased the Providence of God to dispose the matter otherwise, and he is interred in the chapel of the Blessed Virgin, belonging to the house of the Fathers of the Oratory of Saint-Honoré, where many persons of piety come to offer their adorations to the Most Holy and Adorable Trinity at his tomb, not without receiving some special blessing : and for myself, I declare that for many years past—even before I was admitted to the holy ecclesiastical state—I have accounted it a great privilege to go and offer my vows to my God, and my homage and devotion to His most holy Mother, my gracious and most faithful Mistress, at the tomb of this great servant both of the Son and of the Mother. St. Ignatius, the founder of the Company of Jesus, appearing after his death, showed himself enveloped in a cloud ; and Father De Condren also (of whom we have just spoken), on occasion of his appearance, was seen to hide his countenance with a veil, as if these admirable persons were still reluctant to display themselves in their glory : so true is it that there is none but God only who is to be regarded, esteemed, and loved in all things. Ah ! God only, God only, God only.

CHAPTER III.

We ought to Combat in a Christian Way the Inclination we have to Self-Display.

The life of a God-made-man is all admirable ; it is infinitely marvellous. A God comes down from heaven, He is incarnate in the womb of a young

Virgin, He is made man like unto us, with the design of abiding four-and-thirty years among men. Certainly there is no mind but must be lost in an abyss of admiration at the sight of conduct so astonishing on the part of a God. But where is the mind that does not at the same time think that, doubtless, this God-Man comes to lead a life brilliant and glorious in the eyes of all the creatures of this habitable world? And yet He passes thirty years of His life hidden; He remains in the house of a poor carpenter, working with him at his trade. Is the human mind capable of conceiving conduct such as this? God is made man, and of the thirty-four years during which He designs to remain with men, He passes thirty in the workshop of a carpenter! Where shall we find wisdom, learning, or power of intellect capable of comprehending conduct so wonderful? O my Saviour, I see clearly that Thou actest according to Thy Omnipotence when Thou subduest unbelievers to Thy Gospel; for reason cannot rise to the height of Thy ways. We have already spoken of this great truth, and we will still continue to speak of it; nor shall we ever weary of the subject. A God is made man, and He employs Himself in following the trade of a carpenter, with a poor mechanic, nearly all His life, with the exception of the three or four last years which He passed in this world. This is incomprehensible. But, O my soul, let this conduct of thy God instruct us, in the most effectual way, that there must be within us some strange disorder which disposes us to court observation, when a God-Man devotes so much time to the hidden life! Wherefore, it is impossible to doubt but that pride and vanity are the great evils of corrupt nature, seeing that a God applies Himself so earnestly to the destruction of these evils by remedies wholly contrary to them.   This ought to convince us beyond all question that such sins are the most opposed to God, that they make dreadful ravages in souls, and even poison all the good we are able to do; and therefore it is (as we have already observed) that the Son of God abides with us, and will continue to abide with us even to the consummation of ages, that He may make unceasing satisfaction to His Father for the pride and vanity of creatures, and avert from them the great and terrible scourges which they deserve.   Ah! what a marvel, what a miracle of love!   The creature, which is nothingness itself, is ever striving to raise itself; and God, who is the great All, never ceases to annihilate Himself!   These are overwhelming considerations, such as leave no Christian mind any way of escape.   We are under the indispensable necessity, then, of generously combating against the inclination which prompts us to put ourselves forward and court the esteem of men.   This is the great battle which the Christian has to wage; this is the point against which he must direct his arms, or rather, I should say, the arms of our Lord; and it is a battle he must fight all the days of his life, and even to the very moment of his death.   Here there is no truce, and none is admissible; it is a warfare which must be continued even to death.

O Christian soul, fight thou, then, "the battles of the Lord"—to adopt the language of Scripture.   Love, and ever aspire after, the hidden life, in the company of Him who is our gracious Master and our All.   Let us combat the inclination we have to display ourselves both in temporal and spiritual things.   Let us never desire rich clothing, costly furniture, sumptuous repasts, splendid houses, and grand retinue; the ostentation of riches, high offices, worldly credit and power; science, genius, a critical judgment, a retentive memory, eloquence in speech; the esteem, consideration, and friendship of creatures, familiarity and favour with the great, a ready welcome in society, the approbation and applause of men. Let us not of our own accord take upon us any employment or situation of trust, or seek the office of director or preacher, or meddle with works of importance, however good and holy. Let us await in patience the order of God; let us beware, above all, of a natural eagerness which would lead us to attempt a number of good works which the All-Gracious God does not require of us, under the plea of promoting His glory. And here I must point out that it is one of the most dangerous artifices of self-love to cloak itself with a zeal for the glory of God; as a remedy for which it is good to consider two particulars, exceedingly worthy of notice in the life of our Lord, our divine example.

The first is, that He might have performed innumerable good works, from which He nevertheless abstained because such was not the order of His Father. For instance, He might have preached in many kingdoms, and yet He taught only in Judæa and Galilee, and that but for a few years. He might have spent a long life among men, and during all that time have traversed the whole earth and done incalculable good; and yet He died at the age of thirty-four. He had the power of changing metals into gold, and consequently of assisting all the poor throughout the world, and building hospitals in every place; and yet He did nothing of all this, preferring the mean and abject life which He had chosen for Himself to all these great and charitable works.   He could have written and composed books worthy of a God, as He was ; and yet He never chose to do so.   This was the reason which Father De Condren alleged for refusing to write when he was urged to give the world the benefit of the truly angelical lights with which he was endowed.   "Ah !" replied this holy man (as has been already observed), " Jesus, my God, possessed lights far more excellent, more exalted, and more divine, and nevertheless He committed none of them to writing."   This is why I must repeat once more that, while I write these truths, I confess I feel myself covered with shame and confusion—I who am but a handful of dust and a miserable sinner ; and I beseech my Christian brethren who may read these little works, to weep with me over my exceeding unworthiness.   But so it is, that God requires the merest nothings, sinful men, to do what He was not pleased to do Himself.   O my Sovereign Lord, O my Amiable Saviour, it is with this conviction, and having regard only to Thy sacred commands, that I venture to speak and write of Thy divine testimonies. Pardon me, O my Adorable Master, enter not into judgment with Thy poor servant ; for who am I that I should dare to speak or to write of my God ?   O Mother of Mercy, my refuge in all things,—O my good angel guardian,—O all ye nine choirs of holy angels,—and all ye saints of Paradise, obtain mercy for me from the great God of infinite majesty, of whom I have presumed to speak and write.   And besides, it should be observed that the all-gracious God does not always require of us every species of good that might be done ; in this matter we ought to consult those true servants of God who are versed in the science of the saints, that we may not go beyond the order of God, nor on the other hand neglect what we ought to do in accordance therewith. Let us beware of that eagerness which springs from natural activity and self-love, and is ever urging us to some course of action which may make us of importance in the minds of men; and let us avoid on the other hand that indolence, negligence, and tepidity which leads to the disregard of many things which God would have us to do. Happy he who at his death shall be able to repeat those words of our gracious Saviour: "'Father, I have finished the work which Thou gavest Me to do' (John xvii. 4)—I have remained in the solitude in which I was placed by Thee; I have not displayed myself before the eyes of men, seeing that Thou wouldst have me lead a life of retirement; I have preached and heard confessions because Thou didst call me thereto." In fine, there are some whom God calls to a life of complete seclusion. There are others whom He calls to great and almost continual labours, always, however, with the reservation of necessary time for prayer and recollection; others, again, he calls to a mixed life of retirement and intercourse with men, occupying them only at certain times in the service of their neighbour. "There are those," said a holy person of our time, " who are not called to preach whole Lent and Advent courses, but who in the order of God's Providence have to preach occasionally and from time to time;" and the truth of this remark I have myself observed clearly exemplified in many instances.

The second thing to be considered is that we ought not to be eager, out of our own natural activity, to perform even those things which God requires of us. Our Lord, as He Himself testifies (Luke xx. 15), desired with a great desire the work of our redemption, and He declared (xii. 50) that He was even straitened until it should be accomplished; and yet, with all these ineffable desires of the most ardent love with which heart was ever consumed, He did nothing in haste; He did not forestall by one single moment the hour determined by His Father : He even fled away and hid Himself from His enemies because that hour had not yet come. Powerful example to restrain and moderate the inclinations of an impetuous nature. Let us remember also what this Divine Master taught us (Acts i. 7), that it is not for us to know the times or moments which the Father hath put in His own power. Let us bless the Lord meanwhile : He will dispose of the moments, hours, years, times, opportunities, persons, means, and appliances of which we shall have need to accomplish the works which He would have us to do. A young man was urged by his director to take holy orders, and turn his mind to the procuring some place suitable to his vocation. He was also much blamed by his nearest relatives, by many Religious, and other judicious persons, because he did nothing towards providing for himself. He was even ridiculed on this account, but, in spite of all that was said to him, he looked only to the Lord, and placed all his hopes in the protection of the most holy Virgin, the good angels, and the saints, abandoning himself without reserve to the care of Divine Providence, which tended him, and still tends him, like a most kind, gentle, and faithful mother—yea, and suffices him, more satisfied a hundred thousand times while confiding in her merciful goodness, than if all

the crowned heads in the world had undertaken to provide for all his needs. When persons spoke to him of
seeking a provision for himself, he was deeply moved,
and even recoiled with horror from such a proposal.
"Ah!" he would say, "sufficient for me to seek the
interests of God alone, and of His most holy Mother.
Self-interest is an abomination." "But," his director
used to say, "you would be able, by the help of divine
grace, to do much for your neighbour in the situation you might occupy;" to which it was his wont
to reply that his good mother, Divine Providence,
would not fail to furnish him with the opportunity
whenever she required this service of him. And, in
truth, O my God, who has ever hoped in Thee and
been confounded? When nothing was less in his
mind, he was offered an important benefice, which he
accepted, after having refused it during the space of a
year. He assumed this charge in obedience to his
director, who made him come a distance of 150 miles
to undertake it, without acquainting him with the
object of his journey; and what shows that it was a
simple effect of Divine Providence is, that the person
who presented him with this benefice did so entirely
from a disinterested motive, disregarding the solicita-
tions of flesh and blood, which powerfully opposed it,
and forgetting even his own interest by sacrificing
several benefices and dignities which were offered him
on condition of his bestowing the former in accordance
with the anxious wishes of others. O my Saviour
and my God, how happy is the man who has placed
his hope in Thee, desiring only what Thou willest, as
Thou willest, and when Thou willest! Thy designs
shall without doubt be accomplished in him, whatever
opposition earth and hell may raise.

It is related of a great servant of God of our time that these words were one day put into his mind by God : " Care not to be known, neither be solicitous to know." And a sudden illumination caused him to see that herein would be found the greatest aids in the spiritual life. It may, at least, be said with truth that we have within us an inclination to self-display, the offspring of self-love, from which it is difficult to free ourselves ; an inclination to which most men yield, and which taints the purity of all our actions, the best of which are not perfectly exempt from it : and this is sufficient to teach us the obligation we are under of resisting an inclination so universal and so dangerous.

CHAPTER IV.

WE OUGHT CAREFULLY TO AVOID EVERYTHING THAT CAN MINISTER TO DISPLAY.

AFTER we have resolved to combat in a Christian manner the inclinations we have for self-display, arising out of our natural corruption and self-love, we onght in the next place, after the example of our Lord and His saints, to endeavour carefully to avoid everything that can confer distinction upon us, and make us conspicuous in the world. We ought not, therefore, to desire high offices or honourable employments, but, above all, we should beware of soliciting them either in our own person or by means of friends. For this is a human way of acting for which the Spirit of God has always inspired a strong aversion, as is most observable in the lives of saints who have had the largest share in the plenitude of His graces. And it may be truly said that the longing desire felt by people of the world for high offices and dignities has never equalled in intensity the distaste, repugnance, and aversion with which those who possess the Spirit of God have regarded them. For, indeed, the Spirit of Jesus Christ is ever the same; a spirit of humility and self-abasement, of estrangement from all the vain honours of this life, detachment from everything that the world values and loves, attraction towards the hidden life, content to be known simply by God alone; while, on the other hand, the spirit of the world is always seeking those things which procure credit among men and bring distinction to their possessors. Consider, ye who read this, by which of these spirits you are actuated, and then reflect that, when the multitude would have chosen our Lord for their King, as soon as that amiable Saviour perceived their design, He withdrew Himself immediately, and retired into a place apart. Thus did the Adorable Jesus treat the highest honours of earth. O Christian soul, how do we both stand in this matter? Yet saints, who are truly saints only by the conformity of their life with that of their divine model, walking in the steps of this Adorable Master, far from anxiously seeking situations of the highest distinction, either in the ecclesiastical or in the secular state, have used extraordinary efforts to escape them. A St. Gregory is chosen to be Sovereign Pontiff over the whole Church, the highest title in the world; and this man of God flies and hides himself, and it needs that the Omnipotence of God should work miracles in order to draw him from his hiding-place and oblige him to accept the loftiest station upon earth.   All ecclesiastical history is full of such examples; it is impossible to describe the efforts made by saints to avoid possessing anything here below which could confer distinction upon them or give them importance in the eyes of men.   What have they not done to escape all those honours which the world and its followers use every endeavour to attain!   O my God, what a difference between the souls which Thou leadest and those which are led by a human and worldly spirit!   In our own days we have seen Father De Condren take to flight when he was elected general of his Congregation.   But, you will say to me, are not the servants of God called to fill high offices?   Yes, they are so called; but, I reply, they do not make interest for them; they await the order of God; they accept them in fear, and oftentimes not without sighs and tears : for they are grieved to behold themselves summoned to occupy a position which brings them consideration in the world, as they look upon a God-Man abject and despised, who said of Himself that He was " a worm and no man."   O all ye who profess to be His servants have you really fathomed this truth ?

We must carefully avoid all places, persons, and companies, and everything else which give us an interest in the hearts of creatures.   Thus we must not be too ready to associate with the great, or to mix with the clever and fashionable people of the day, or to contract habits of intimacy with those who are themselves distinguished in the world, or who reflect distinction upon others.   We must shun the flattery, the praise, and the applause of men.   Father De

Condren, whom we mention so often, used to make his escape when he had succeeded in some affair at court, which sometimes was the case in a very striking manner, and in important matters which concerned the first personages of the realm and the welfare of the State. Being a man filled with the Spirit of Jesus Christ, he felt so great an aversion for the praises of men, that he could not endure to hear them. Oh, how melancholy to see persons of piety, who perform many good works when they are noticed by the world, and while their self-love finds its gratification in the familiar intercourse and friendship of the creatures with whom they associate, yet seem to lose all power of working when the esteem and friendship of creatures are wanting! Oh, how pitiable to be always wishing to see and be seen! But happy they who are content with God alone! Happy those preachers and directors who announce the Gospel, the ways of Jesus Christ, to neglected multitudes in remote places, where the gay world never comes, where the confessionals are not besieged with satin and finery; who teach " with all patience and doctrine " (2 Tim. iv. 2),—and, indeed, much is needed with rough country people, who have little intellect, little memory, and much rudeness of manner, where nature meets with nothing to flatter it, but everything to repel and disgust it. And here I would entreat with tears those many preachers and directors who are almost unneeded in large towns, or do but little there, to take pity on so many perishing souls, which have cost the blood and the life of a God, not only amongst the heathen—although the case of idolatrous countries is more urgent, and more may there be done for the glory of God, for there it is question of conquering whole empires to our Divine Saviour—but also amongst the multitudes who are eternally lost for want of help in so many places, in our own native France, which are destitute of evangelical labourers, and where the people in the midst of Christianity scarcely know what it is to be Christians.

But to return to our subject : we may say that self-love mixes itself up so commonly with everything that brings us into notice, that those souls which have been most eminent in sanctity have used every means to shelter themselves from it, and to avoid everything, however trifling, which could draw attention to them.   This it is that inspired them with such utter aversion, not only for the vain distinctions of the world, but for all that could in any way lead thereto. Father De Condren, when he was only about seven years old, but full, even at so early an age, of the Spirit of God, on seeing a likeness that had been taken of him, for he was possessed of great personal beauty, could not endure the sight of it, young as he was, and had no rest until he had torn it to pieces. Certain treatises had been dedicated by their authors to that great servant of God, Father Mataincourt, then general of the Congregation of our Saviour of the Canons Regular of Lorraine ; but as soon as the man of God observed his own picture in the frontispiece he ordered the person who had dedicated them to him, who was one of his own religious, to bring him all the copies, without telling him his object, and, animated by a holy severity, seized a knife and cut and tore them into fragments ; so filled was he with that holy Evangelical hatred which the Son of God so much recommends to us, and which He so powerfully inculcated on His disciples. So far, indeed, were these holy persons from any desire to have their portraits taken, that on the contrary they would have rejoiced to be effaced from the memory of every living creature. At the sight of these examples, and of so many others, given by persons who had attained to the highest eminence in the ways of divine love, what can be said by those who try to make themselves live in the esteem and memory of men, not only during their life but after their death, in every possible way, and who carry this to such an excess as even to affix their coat of arms on sacred chalices, chasubles, altars, and other most holy things?

They who have been truly moved by the Spirit of Jesus Christ, have sought only spiritual annihilation in all things. Hence it is that they have had recourse to so many holy artifices to keep out of sight everything that could make them of consequence in the world, either on the score of birth, personal advantages, and natural talents, or on account of their graces, virtues, and extraordinary gifts. I allow that the Spirit of God has sometimes impelled them to speak of their interior, and disclose the special mercies bestowed upon them by the divine goodness, the Providence of God so disposing for His own glory and the good of souls. But, in truth, this has been the result of a particular guidance and by the movement of a special interior grace; for, speaking generally, the saints have maintained a very strict silence on the subject of their graces; and, if sometimes they have suffered anything to escape them, it has been mostly through inadvertence; and they have been covered with confusion and greatly afflicted when they reflected on what they had done, and it has been the occasion of much humiliation to them; and, after all, in spite of all the pains that have been taken to obtain some knowledge of their graces, and notwithstanding all that they may have themselves said, what was greatest and the most divine in their interior life has remained unknown to men.   One who desires to make some progress in pure love, ought not to be forward to speak of the graces he has received or anything else calculated to excite esteem.   Our Lord gives us a most admirable example in this matter : if He allows a ray of His glory to appear, it is only to three of His most beloved disciples, in a retired place apart ; and even then He commands them to keep the glorious vision secret ; nay, it would seem as if He wished to efface the recollection of it from the minds of those who beheld it, for immediately He discourses to them of the shame and sufferings of His Passion. One of the great maxims of the spiritual life is to speak little, especially of the trifling good we may be able to do.   Moses, in the book of Exodus (iv. 10), declares that his difficulty of speech had increased from the time that he had enjoyed the privilege of conversing with God.   They who talk the most are often the least recollected.   The soul that is fully occupied interiorly is loth to display itself externally ; it is satisfied with the knowledge which God possesses of what passes within, and of the good it is able to do through His mercy ; it says nothing thereof to creatures, for it hopes nothing and expects nothing from them : such conduct is strongly recommended by the Gospel, which teaches us to pray in secret, and forbids us to attract attention when we give alms, or be of a sorrowful countenance when we fast, that so we may repress the inclinations of corrupt nature, which are ever prompting us to court the observation of the world. Not that the Son of God condemns public prayers, seeing that He Himself sanctioned them by frequenting the Temple services, or good works which may serve to the edification of others; but what He wishes to teach us, is that we can never be sufficiently on our guard against a secret self-love, which bears sway within us, and is always inclining us to make ourselves of consequence in the eyes of men. But how touching do these truths become in the admirable examples which this Heavenly Master has given us of them! Surely He might have delivered the most eloquent, the most divine discourses during the whole of His hidden life, and yet He did not. His most glorious Mother observed the same manner of life, as did also the glorious St. Joseph, her virginal spouse. In fine, He accomplished our salvation and consummated His most glorious work, not in a series of brilliant achievements, but in ways the most hidden, even in the agonies of an ignominious death. "Wonderful thought!" exclaims St. Augustine; "He is not glorified when He raises the dead, an act surpassingly glorious in the eyes of the world, and He is glorified when He dies the death of a malefactor, which the world esteems as the depth of infamy." Oh, how full of consolation are these truths to such as are persecuted, crucified, whose very crosses seem to render them useless to the world! But how convincingly ought they to teach those whose state in life obliges them to be great in the eyes of the world, not to value themselves on that account; the divine word even teaching us that "that which is high to men is an abomination before God" (Luke xvi. 15). Oh, how unlike are God's ways to our ways!

CHAPTER V.

We ought to observe a constant watchfulness over ourselves by the faithful practice of mortification in those situations wherein by the Providence of God we are obliged to put ourselves forward.

Having considered the indispensable necessity by which we are bound to combat our inclination to self-display, and the obligation we are under of avoiding as much as possible everything that might minister to display, we must observe in the next place that we ought to watch over ourselves with all possible diligence when, by the Providence of God, we are obliged to put ourselves forward. It was the opinion of the great St. Francis of Sales that it was easier to refrain from being angry, than, being angry, to maintain that just moderation which Christianity demands of us. And for my part, if it is permitted me to express my poor opinion, I believe that it is more easy to decline situations of honour, and to refrain from such actions as make a noise in the world and excite the esteem of men, than to keep out self-love when we occupy such situations and perform such actions. Persons may, indeed, be found living in retirement and solitude, who, contented with their lot, have no desire to be known; others again may be met with, despised and persecuted by the world, who care nothing for its contempt and ill-usage, and desire none of its honours and rewards. And for this reason, we may remark in passing, it is a precious grace to have some share in a life of retirement, humiliation, and reproach, and we ought to bless our Lord, His holy Mother, and the good angels for it. But where is the man whose position or whose actions bring him consideration in the world, who does not feel some secret complacency therein, or derive some almost imperceptible satisfaction from the honours that are paid him? O my God, how dangerous is it, then, to be much considered, esteemed, and loved by creatures! How great a misfortune is it to be applauded and praised, to meet only with those who commend what we say and do, and to receive nothing but civilities, and flattering compliments, and marked attentions in society and from persons with whom we associate! How sad to be everywhere well received in the world, to be surrounded on all sides with those who honour and caress you, and say a thousand things in your praise, and make great interest for you, and set you up in the good opinions of others! In truth, I tremble, I greatly tremble, when I see a man universally esteemed and loved; and the reason is this: when I read the Gospel, which to me and all sincere Christians is indubitable and infallible truth, I find that our most gracious God and Master promises the very opposite to His dearest friends, and that such a life is utterly unlike that of our Divine Saviour, His holy Mother, and His true disciples.

However, as there are faithful servants of our

gracious Lord and Master who are truly called to fill distinguished offices—and indeed none other ought to occupy such positions, especially the highest dignities of the Church, to which only those who are perfect ought to be raised, seeing that they are states that presuppose an already attained perfection—as there are, then, in these situations, persons whose virtue is commended, and who enjoy a high reputation for sanctity; and as all these things happen according to God's appointment, who disposes them to His own ends and for His own greater glory; they must not leave the path along which they are led, since it is chosen for them by the good pleasure of God; for we are all along supposing this, having no intention of favouring in any way those persons who have chosen their state in life or their occupations from mere natural motives, human respect, or self-interest. Abiding, then, in the state in which the Providence of God has placed us, we must be constantly on the watch to destroy every admixture of nature, and to act only from the movements of grace, without mingling therewith human aims or mere natural motives.

To this end we ought especially to consider, making it the subject of deep and serious reflection, and that not transiently and cursorily, but frequently, as, for instance, several times a week, even choosing besides some stated time, at least once a month—we ought to consider, I say, the very great danger such a state of life involves by reason of the corruption of our nature. O my God, who can ever speak too strongly of it? who can ever think sufficiently of it? Alas! was it not the knowledge of this danger that caused the greatest saints to make incredible efforts to avoid such a state? Woe unto us, who not only seek it, but pursue it with such pitiable eagerness! Truly, truly, it is more difficult than men suppose to persevere therein in the faithful and constant practice of pure virtue; for it is evident that riches have a strangely corrupting effect on their possessors; which effect comes not from the riches themselves, for God made nothing that was not good, but from our own evil inclinations, which cause us to love them and cling closely to them, as experience teaches us every day, and sometimes in the case even of those who make profession of more than usual devotion: for it is most astonishing to see persons of piety so eager after wealth; so anxious to acquire more, although they already possess much; so tenacious of their rights in the smallest matters, sometimes even going to law for some little plot of ground; such thrifty managers in saving up money. These people really seem to fear that their daily bread will fail them, and find the greatest difficulty in trusting to Divine Providence: they are hard in all their money transactions, doling out their workmen's wages with a niggardly exactness, and never paying a farthing beyond what they have engaged to do; sooner than spare a penny or some trifling sum which they are unwilling to give, because they are not strictly bound to do so, they would endure to see God outraged before their eyes by the impatience, murmurs, and imprecations of those whom they thus disappoint; they grudge every little expense which they are obliged to incur; it is true they give alms (for I am speaking of those who make profession of devotion), but they leave undone a thousand good works they might have done, and sometimes even such as they are bound to do, though the omission does not strike them because of the blindness with which they are afflicted; and, after all, they think they have done wonders when they have parted with some small portion out of a hundred things, the whole of which they might easily have bestowed upon charitable works.   I declare that, after an attentive consideration of such conduct on the part of a number of persons possessed of worldly goods, who, nevertheless, endeavour to serve God, practise meditation, frequent the sacraments, read nothing but good books, descant admirably on the maxims of the Gospel, are especially loud in the praises of poverty, often repeating, "Blessed are the poor," and "Woe to those who are rich," according to the infallible words of Jesus Christ—after such considerations, I have the strongest possible conviction that the possession of riches is more dangerous than words can express; for if such are the miserable results in the case of persons so enlightened, and who even give themselves to the service of God, what must we think of the danger of those rich men who are not in these good dispositions?   And so, if you consider, you will see that from the beginning of the Gospel dispensation God has made use of the poor, for instance, the Apostles, or of those who, being rich, have embraced poverty, to accomplish His greatest designs for the publication of His truth and the reformation of manners.   I will mention another fact which I have often remarked in families which were either poor or but little provided with the goods of this world: I have seen a wonderful liberality, a charity which I have not words to describe, a care for the interests of others, which was the source of much general edification; for, far from exhibiting that grudging disposition which I have mentioned as so characteristic of the rich, they evinced such readiness in paying those whom they employed, and such liberality in remunerating them for any little work they might have done for them, that these persons were extremely edified by their treatment of them. I say, then, that as there is very great danger in riches, even to persons of piety, there is no less danger in those states which are attended with worldly esteem, reputation, and honour : and this is so true that we see those who are full of good desires and right intentions, who promise great things, and excite high expectations of the good they will effect in Church and State, who possess a tender conscience and evince a horror of sin ; and who, nevertheless, are no sooner elevated to some honourable position or obtain a great reputation in the world, than they sink into a state of frightful tepidity, followed by such blindness of heart as effectually hides from their eyes their most pressing obligations, and makes them insensibly fall in with the maxims of the world and live like the multitude around them. The great business of their life is to keep a good table and maintain a large establishment ; to have their houses well furnished, and be surrounded with company ; to talk of what is going on in the world, and contrive how they may rise to still greater distinction, and preserve and increase the consideration to which they have attained : but as for the momentous subject of Eternity, and the truths of the Gospel, and the maxims of the Son of God, these things are little in their thoughts ; they no longer think of attending to mental prayer, or to the practice of Christian mortification and pure virtue, or of self-renunciation and the love of the cross. This is why, I repeat, we ought first of all to consider the very great danger in which we stand.

In the second place, after considering seriously and frequently the extreme danger of such a state, we must walk therein with fear and trembling, like those who tread on the brink of a precipice, lest, forgetting to look to our steps, we slip and fall headlong. Ah! how many persons occupying a high position have been lost for want of this fear! how many preachers and directors, how many who were of great repute in both the ecclesiastical and the secular state! Let us call to mind the great Apostle, let us consider his divine, his miraculous vocation, his exaltation to the third heaven, the gifts and favours that were lavished upon him, but above all his life so innocent, yea so divine, for he lived only by the life of Jesus (Gal. ii. 20); and then let us remember how he exclaims (1 Cor. ix. 27) that he fears lest he should become a castaway. With such an example before your eyes, you must be presumptuous indeed, no matter who you may be, if you do not feel yourself encompassed with dangers and are not seized with a great fear.

In the third place, we must not abandon ourselves unreservedly to the circumstances of our state: it is this, above all, that has caused the ruin of so many in a like condition. I mean that we must live therein with a simple regard to the will of God, taking care not to allow ourselves to be engrossed by the pleasures and honours incidental to our position. Be occupied, then, with your state as much as God requires of you, but nothing more. Beware of forming connections and friendships, not only such as are worldly, but even such as are simply natural. Shun the society of men of the world, for they will corrupt you. You will be seized with a desire to have splendid equipages like them, to live sumptuously as they do, to indulge in the same gaieties; or, if your means do not allow of such things, at least you will adopt the spirit and air of the world. Fly frivolous amusements, prolonged conversations; contrive to have time for prayer and retirement, and the reading of books, not only doctrinal, but devotional. Be assured that no excuses are admissible in this matter. Do you not find time for eating and sleeping?

In the fourth place, do what the all-gracious God requires of you according to your state, and nothing more. I admit you are called to an active life, but do not exceed the bounds marked out for you by the Providence of God; for otherwise this is what happens: We so exhaust ourselves by our exterior exertions that interiorly we become dry, and even lose the habit of recollection. The Spirit of God departs, a human spirit enters in, and after that, a worldly spirit. Persons thus affected gradually decline from the purity of the evangelical maxims, they acquire a relish for those of the world, and attempt to serve two masters, although the Son of God has declared it to be impossible. They desire to accommodate the principles of the Gospel to those of the world. I repeat, then: contrive to have leisure for prayer and retirement, and occasionally provide for yourselves some place of retreat into which you may withdraw for a season. Wherefore you must take heed to these two things: not to give yourselves to exterior action more than God requires of you; and, when engaged therein in the order of His Divine providence, not to throw yourselves into it with eagerness.   Oh, how necessary is the sense of the Presence of God to restrain us from such unguarded effusion!

In the fifth place, be not forward to speak of the successes with which God favours you, your reputation, your circle of friends and acquaintance, your influence.   As much as is possible, suffer nothing to appear which can bring you into notice.   Avoid paying visits to the great, or pay them in as private a manner as possible; if they are necessary, choose a time when you are not likely to be observed.   Speak little of your own talents or natural abilities, and judiciously divert the conversation when you are yourself the subject of it.   Do not take pleasure in hearing others talk of your preaching, or of the good you may do, or of anything which is to your credit.   I will say more : do not willingly think of these things; for it is difficult to occupy the mind with any success we have had, without taking some secret complacency therein. We must refer everything to God, and ascribe to Him all the good we may effect by sermons, or in the discharge of our official duties, whether ecclesiastical or civil; and this we shall be able to do with the divine assistance; putting from us all thoughts that terminate in ourselves, that lead us to contemplate ourselves in the good we do, or to reflect on what people think or say of us; and directing all our thoughts to God alone, looking to Him only, His glory and His divine interests, in total forgetfulness of everything that regards ourselves.

In the sixth place, remember that our life is a continual warfare even to the very moment of death. Be assured, then, once for all, that we must continually fight, and that without intermission ; and bear in mind that many have for years generously resisted that inclination to self-display and that desire of admiration which comes of this ill-regulated self-love— that many have persevered for a long time in the love of the hidden life, entertaining a holy contempt for the esteem and affection of creatures, caring only to be known of God alone—who in the end have fallen into a state of great relaxation ; for the inconstancy of man exceeds all bounds, so difficult is it for him to remain steadfast in any one state. Wherefore our advice is that you never cease to maintain the strictest watch over yourselves in those situations which oblige you to put yourselves forward, and walk circumspectly and in great fear, as has been already said, seeing how rare is perseverance in such circumstances. O my God, what a pitiable sight do creatures present who are so easily attracted by trifles, and so often fall when an occasion of sin presents itself, and so eagerly attach themselves to whatever is pleasing in their own eyes or adds to their credit in those of others !

Finally, if in these exalted states and amidst these honourable employments you are opposed, censured, despised, and deserted, you ought to make it a subject of inexpressible joy, seeing that opposition, contempt, repulse, and desertion are the great means of which Divine Providence makes use, to hide the good we are able to effect with the grace of our merciful Saviour, and under the protection of the most glorious Virgin, our good Mother and Mistress, the good angels, and the saints. Oh, exalted and most blessed lot ! to do great works for the glory of God and of His holy Mother, to succeed in our undertakings with the blessing of Heaven, to look simply to the interests of God alone; and yet to pass for a self-interested person, who possesses no great talents and meets with little success, and so to be lightly esteemed and little commended, nay, despised and repelled.

———

CHAPTER VI.

WE OUGHT TO PRACTISE MUCH SELF-HUMILIATION, AND ENDURE WITH RELUCTANCE THE ESTEEM AND FRIENDSHIP OF CREATURES.

SOME may be astonished at what I am about to say; but nevertheless it is a great truth, which will be acknowledged by all holy souls whom our Lord has enlightened with His true light, that there is nothing more afflicting or more humiliating in this life to a sincere Christian than to see himself regarded with esteem and friendship by the world. Many truths to which we have drawn attention in this little work render it impossible to gainsay this opinion. But I will repeat here, what I have already said, that the approbation, the applause, and the friendship of the world give us but little resemblance to our Divine Master and Sacred Model, or, rather, they establish so great a diversity between our state and His most holy life, that it is difficult indeed under such circumstances to find much comfort. It was once said by our Divine Lord that the servant is not greater than his master, and that the world which had persecuted Him would persecute His disciples also (John xv. 20). After so express a testimony from the mouth of a God, what shall we do, or what can we think, when we see ourselves surrounded with honour and glory? "If I please men," exclaims the great Apostle, "I should not be the servant of Jesus Christ" (Gal. i. 10). If, then, we please men, what can we think of ourselves, and what is our state? "All who will live piously in Christ Jesus," declares the same Apostle (2 Tim. iii. 12), "shall suffer persecution." If, then, we are not persecuted, how can we imagine that we live piously? A holy bishop, entering the house of a wealthy man, who had never known what it was to be afflicted, and was held in high estimation and honour by the world, no sooner became aware of the prosperous condition of this man, rich in what men count riches, than he fled away, exclaiming that the curse of heaven was upon one so blessed by earth; and history relates that within a very short time he was crushed under the ruins of his house. It is a favourite maxim of the saints that it is most difficult to be well off in this world and in the next. They who are well to do in this life ought to stand in great fear lest they should have their reward here below. The Grand Turk has driven our Lord from his land, and destroyed His holy religion; and, after all, what earthly advantages does he lack? He is one of the great lords of the earth, and there is none that lives amidst greater pleasures. Filled and penetrated with these thoughts, Father De Condren used to wonder greatly that Divine Providence had withheld from him these great honours and pleasures of the world; for, said he, "My sins, indeed, deserved that I should be given over to the ways of the world, which are ways of pleasure, riches, and honours in this present life." St. Francis Borgia, seeing himself held in honour, cried out, "Alas! to what have my sins brought me!" regarding the esteem and friendship of the world among the chief scourges of God.

"Ah!" exclaimed a holy soul, "must we possess so large a share of that of which Jesus had so little?" The saints were filled with shame, and confusion covered their face, when they beheld themselves honoured where Jesus had appeared only as a worm of the earth and the reproach of men. And surely we may well die of shame when we call to mind His state in the world, and contrast it with our own! A holy servant of God was wont to say that the more souls were banished from the hearts of creatures, the nearer they were brought to the Heart of God. Oh, blessed is the soul which renounces all this love of the creature, all the tender affections and flattering caresses of men, that it may taste the sweetness of Jesus, who is rejected and expelled from the hearts of the worldly. "My kingdom," said this amiable Saviour, "is not of this world" (John xviii. 36). Oh, what happiness, then, not to reign, but to suffer humiliation with Him here! This is the sure way to become partakers in the never-ending glory of His eternal kingdom; for, as Holy Scripture expressly declares (Acts xiv. 21), "we must enter into this kingdom of God through many tribulations." "If," said the Adorable Jesus to St. Catherine of Siena, "if thou wouldst wear the golden crown of the blessed in Paradise, thou must wear the crown of thorns of the afflicted in this present life." Deeply affected by these considerations, the late Father John Chrysostom, religious penitent of the Third Order of St. Francis, longed only for humiliation and contempt; nay, he was enamoured thereof with such a holy fervour that he made a vow to fast a hundred days in honour of the Blessed St. Joseph, if through his powerful patronage he might obtain the precious grace of being despised by all mankind. And more than this, he bound himself by vow to use every means in his power, without departing from the order of God's providence, to draw upon himself the contempt of creatures. That holy man, Father John of the Cross, was so entirely possessed by the same sentiments that when our Lord desired him to choose what he would as a reward for his arduous labours, the only recompense which he begged this all-gracious God to bestow upon him, was that he might suffer and be despised, that the afflictions and crosses which he already endured might be continued or increased. Other holy souls have adopted other measures in order to deprive themselves of the esteem and friendship of creatures ; for instance, that admirable virgin of whom history relates that, while serving in a community which did not keep enclosure, and living in the practice of the most exalted virtue, without giving any exterior tokens of her eminent sanctity, God was pleased to make her known in some extraordinary manner, that she immediately took to flight, without any one being able to tell whither she had gone. And here I would ask whether there is an ambitious man in the world who pursues glory with as much ardour as this holy virgin sought after the hidden and obscure life. But it is something still more wonderful to behold a St. Alexis, who, though it was the Blessed Virgin herself who made him known, so that he could not doubt, after such an intimation from heaven, that it had happened according to the providence of God, nevertheless, immediately took to flight, and withdrew from a place where, if he was known to men, it was only through the personal revelation of the glorious Mother of God.

But, in fact, souls closely united with Jesus find it an insupportable burden to see themselves treated with consideration in a world in which this amiable God-Man led a mean, obscure, and friendless life, and appeared as a poor stranger. Hence it is that the more lights and graces we receive, the stronger does our inclination for the hidden life become. Let us encourage ourselves, then, as said the late M. de Renty, to love this life all unknown and hidden from the eyes of men, stripping ourselves, and driving from our mind so many superfluous things, so many trifles, which, for all their apparent insignificance, are so greatly injurious, occupying it, as they do, in the place of God. For when I come to consider what it is that interrupts and fritters away this holy, this sweet, this most loving union which we ought to have with God, I find that it is Monsieur this, or Madame that, a conversation—something, at any rate, which for us is a folly. Alas! it is too true that man is such a miserable being that a trifle is sufficient to fill his mind and heart. And, if this be so, has he not every reason to fear when he sees himself surrounded with the honours and riches of this world? Oh! how deeply ought they to humble themselves who are so richly endowed with all that the world esteems and loves, as personal beauty and other natural attractions, the goods of fortune, and worldly rank; for these are generally so many chains binding us lamentably to creatures and keeping us at a distance from the Creator. How many have been lost through attachments which their beauty has caused! how many have been saved by being deprived of it, as well as by other misfortunes which have befallen them!

CHAPTER VII.

WE OUGHT TO REJOICE GREATLY IN BEING UNKNOWN.

IF we ought to be grieved and humbled at finding ourselves esteemed and admired, certainly we have every reason to rejoice when we remain unknown. Nay, I will go so far as to say, that if men knew the value and the excellence of the hidden life, they could not refrain from breaking forth into transports of holy joy. Yes, if there be such a thing as true joy in the world, it is the hidden Christian who possesses it. The hidden life is an inestimable treasure; if men did but know its real worth they would give anything, they would sell everything, to obtain it. Indeed, we may confidently affirm it to be a thing highly esteemed of God, seeing that He so constantly disposes events to that end, even working miracles to bestow it upon men. The lives of the saints supply us with admirable examples of this kind. Happy, then, are we if we walk in the ways which hide us from the eyes of men!

We ought, therefore, greatly to rejoice when we live concealed, and our very existence is unknown to men. It is related of M. de Renty, that he desired to be known by no one on earth, and would have accounted it a gain had people been ignorant that there was any such person in the world; that he would have taken a singular pleasure in being banished from the hearts of all and remaining unknown to every creature. It is a happiness, if we cannot be entirely unknown, at least to be unthought of. It is a very precious grace not to be much esteemed; and this is one wonderful advantage that results from natural defects, want of talents, deficiency in ability and address, poverty, the contempt and desertion of creatures, exclusion from offices and honours. O my brother, far from fretting, be glad and rejoice, if thou art but ill endowed with natural perfections of body and mind, the goods of fortune or temporal honours; only make a Christian use of these deprivations, and, behold! thou art in the royal road of a glorious eternity, far removed from all the dangers incurred by the witty and the beautiful, the rich and the great, who stand on the brink of a precipice. Rejoice if, possessing great talents, they pass unnoticed; if you are cast aside as a useless thing, and are turned to no account. Rejoice if you are not treated with the respect due to your state and position; if your merits do not meet with the consideration they deserve; if you are neither promoted nor rewarded in return for your many services; if, when you might justly have looked to be selected for some office or honorable employment, you are passed over and forgotten; or, although remembered and proposed, are nevertheless rejected; if, when you have laboured meritoriously in promoting some great work of charity, and when even it is to you that, after God and in God, the credit of success is due, the honour of it is nevertheless given to others, and you are yourself utterly disregarded in the matter.   Rejoice if you are slighted and despised; if your presence is not sought at assemblies; if no one asks your advice, or takes counsel of you, or places confidence in you, or treats you otherwise than with reserve, or speaks to you on matters in which you are well versed and ought to take a part; if you are not called to co-operate in brilliant undertakings, or to share in great designs; if you have no access to distinguished circles, or to the acquaintance of persons of rank or merit; if no one visits you; if in company people pay you no attention, or leave you to yourself, or give no heed to you if you make a remark; if everybody avoids you, and you are left to take the lowest place; if on all such occasions you find yourself neglected and treated as though you were nobody; if no one pays you any civility, and that at times when there is every reason to the contrary; and if all this befalls you at the hands of good people, persons of piety, ecclesiastics and religious, as well as others, nay, your very confessor, or director, your own friends and relations, and those who are under obligation to you—I will say more, on the part of servants, attendants, and the lowest of the low; if you meet with all this in spiritual avocations as well as in temporal, and that, too, on occasions, and in situations and employments, where you seem to be singled out for such treatment everybody else receiving due attention.   O Christian soul, I must pause here, and tell you that treatment so repugnant to nature is one of the holiest, the sweetest, the most loving dispensations of Divine Providence in your regard.   Would to God that you did but know the inestimable treasure contained in everything that keeps us at a distance from creatures !   No, I say it

without exaggeration, it can neither be expressed nor
conceived, for it is the great means of possessing God
Only.   And who shall ever fully comprehend what it
is for a soul, a mind, a heart, to possess God Only ?

But let us fathom these hidden ways more deeply.
It is an unspeakable mercy to be unknown to men, or,
if known, to be forgotten by them.   It is an unspeakable mercy, if we are noticed at all, that we should be
treated like persons of no consequence, without civility
and without honour ; that we should be thrust on one
side and made no use of, or deprived of whatever
trifling office we happen to hold ; that we should be
neglected and abandoned for our lack of popular
talents.   But there are still higher ways, so precious
that we may well call them the greatest favours which
our Lord and His blessed Mother bestow on those
who are dearest to them.   These ways are ways of
contempt and opprobrium, which cause us to be more
closely hidden in the most populous cities, than are
the most solitary hermits in the wildest deserts.   Oh,
how completely is the holiest life hidden by slanders
and calumnies, which are able to destroy the best-
established reputation !   It is then, indeed, that the
most solid virtue is unknown, when it passes for mere
hypocrisy.   Turn to the Lives of the Saints, and contemplate St. Marina, who lived and died with her
reputation blackened with the foulest calumny : can
anything be conceived more perfectly hidden ?
Methinks, all who suffer humiliation ought to have a
special devotion to this great saint.   The Blessed
Henry Suso, whose precious death took place on the
25th of January, was hidden indeed, when the vilest
and most dreadful crimes were imputed to him ; as,
for instance, impurity, theft, and magic.   And this

was after the Amiable Jesus had appeared to him, who, changing his name from Henry to Amand, which signifies one who deserves to be loved, immediately caused him to pass through these ways of ignominy; as if this Adorable Master would teach us that it is by these ways that He conducts those who are the most acceptable in His divine eyes, making those walk therein whom He loves the most. Henry Suso was at all times an object of His special mercies; but when He would exalt him to be one of His most favoured saints, abjection and abasement were the means He employed to make him partaker in the divinest communications of His love. We may well believe that these favours were granted him through the influence of the most holy Virgin, for whom this saintly man had an extraordinary devotion, breathing only her pure love. In fine, where is the anchorite who is so hidden as was the Adorable Jesus Himself, expiring ignominiously on a gibbet? Let me say, then, with one of the holy servants of this Divine Saviour, Bless the Eternal Father, if He is pleased to continue on in you the hidden life of His Son; if you are unknown, persecuted, and despised; and give yourselves up to Him that you may keep and maintain it generously, purely, and perseveringly. He who aspires to spend an eternity with Jesus, easily despises the vain creatures of this world.

CHAPTER VIII.

WE OUGHT TO MAKE A HOLY USE OF THE INTERIOR SUFFERINGS WHICH HIDE US FROM OURSELVES.

A GENUINE love of the hidden life does not stop short at those means which hide us from men, it is not satisfied until it has the happiness of remaining hidden even from itself. This it is that makes it prize those states of interior suffering which, depriving it of the knowledge of all the good which the Spirit of God works in the inmost recesses of the soul, leaves it nothing but the sight of its own weaknesses and miseries. In truth, there are certain interior pains which have the effect of entirely hiding those who endure them; for they cause them to pass for persons of little understanding or weak intellect, and at the same time conceal the very virtues themselves, which fall into discredit on account of the little esteem attaching to those who practise them. Sometimes even this ignorance extends to directors and confessors, who still further distress these afflicted persons and serve only to augment their sufferings. In fine, these states not only hide the person who endures them from all earthly creatures, and sometimes from the very angels of heaven; but, more than this, they hide the soul from itself, leaving it under the eye of

God alone.' It would be most difficult for me to express the purity and the excellence of the states I am describing. That purity is truly admirable, the actions of such a person being no longer tainted with those selfish views, those secret self-complacencies, those almost imperceptible feelings of satisfaction, which are the result of the knowledge we have and the reflections we make respecting the good that is being wrought in us. It is well distinctly to note this truth, and convince ourselves once for all, that the clear consciousness of our own virtues and good works, which is accompanied with reflections thereon, exposes us to a great danger of making a sad mixture of the corruption of nature and the sanctity of grace. Sometimes people imagine they are doing wonders; they think they have made great progress in the supernatural life; they fancy that their state is rarely to be equalled; they esteem themselves something, although they are nothing. It is not easy to contemplate self, without self-love and self-interest insinuating themselves to a very great extent. And this is why the Divine Spouse tells His beloved to turn away her eyes from Him, for they have made Him flee away. He means that the looks with which He regards her being followed in her by a secret self-complacency, she is attracted to the consideration of herself; for the more she gives her attention to what concerns herself or her own interests, the further she withdraws herself from perfect union with her Heavenly Spouse. Whence it is, that to heal her of her most secret disorders, and to deliver her from imperfections which are almost hidden from herself, although they are occasioned by her own fault, He diverts her attention from the good that is being wrought in her own interior, and veils all the graces He bestows upon her in a holy obscurity. He opens her eyes to her own miseries; He makes her feel her own weaknesses; He allows her passions to rebel; He suffers her to be assailed with violent and humiliating temptations, and to be grievously tried by devils. To her it appears as if He had deserted her; she seems no longer to have faith, hope, or charity, but to be abandoned by God; she sees nothing before her but punishment and hell; she is tormented with scruples, with doubts whether she has consented to temptations; and sometimes she fancies that she has really given her full consent to them, though in truth she is far removed from anything of the kind. She would wish to be always repeating her confessions, or making a general one anew. She is reluctant to approach the sacraments; she believes all to be lost. As we have treated this subject more at large in our book of " The Holy Ways of the Cross," as well as in that of " The Kingdom of God in Mental Prayer," we shall content ourselves with what we have here touched upon with respect to these states of interior suffering. But one word of encouragement we will give to those who undergo them, viz., that these excruciating states preserve the gifts of God in their purity, and prevent what is most precious in itself from being contaminated with the poison of self-love. In the next place, they prepare the way for the purest state of divine union, they lay the foundation of the holiest ways of grace, and exalt the soul to inconceivable glory in a blessed eternity. Oh, happy those souls that are thus afflicted! Take courage, all ye that are crucified by these sufferings; beware of grieving or disquieting yourselves on account of a state which is a result of the sweetest mercies of God. If you cannot perceive the good it brings with it, at least humble yourselves, and, without trusting to your own lights, which reveal to you nothing but perplexity and distress, trust to the true and solid lights of the saints, who teach you that this state is the great means of uniting you perfectly with God, though it seems to you far otherwise. I do not expect that you should understand your state, or comprehend its blessedness, in the midst of your present darkness; for how is it possible to see amidst the deep shades of a gloomy night? But what I do expect is, that you should submit your mind to the teaching of those who have been illuminated with the purest lights of the Holy Spirit. By thus submitting your understanding, you will learn that what is now the subject of distress and disquietude, ought rather to be matter to you of rejoicing. Oh! would to God that you did but know the treasure you possess. Ah! if ever you attain to heaven, the region of light, you will clearly understand what an advantage it was to you to be deprived of your own natural lights, to walk in the midst of the thickest gloom, to be denied all sensible consolations, whether divine or human, and to endure all the sufferings of which we have spoken. Ah! what thanksgivings will you render to the divine goodness. Begin, then, to do now what you are to do everlastingly, although now you do not comprehend what you will clearly know in a blessed eternity.

However, if you still say that your case is one of such extraordinary suffering that you know not how to support it with patience, I reply that the heaviest crosses are the greatest favours that Heaven bestows upon its choicest favourites. I say, then, that should you suffer the sharpest trials which it is possible to endure, even to being assaulted or possessed by devils, cease not to bless the ways of Divine Providence, ways ever infinitely adorable, ever infinitely amiable, whatever thoughts you may have to the contrary. Ah! cast your eyes upon a God-Man, and behold Him transported by the devil from the desert where He was into the Holy City; see Him carried up by that evil spirit to the pinnacle of the Temple, and from thence borne away to the summit of a high mountain; see how he conducts Him, how he makes Him go whithersoever he will. This consideration, which is one of the truths of faith which it has pleased God should be expressly recorded in the Gospel, and which the Church teaches to all the faithful, is more than sufficient to convince us that there is no state, however hard and humiliating, which we ought not to endure with meekness, with joyfulness, and with thanksgiving. And if you still tell me that what afflicts you most is the darkness which encompasses you, and which neither permits you to discern any good in your sufferings nor leaves you any signs of the presence of God's grace within you, I reply that you thus betray your self-love, although it disguises itself under fair pretexts; for if the love of God were strong within, could you desire aught else but what He wills? Are you ignorant that it is one of His dispensations that no one should know whether he be worthy of love or hatred? In this state, then, we must abide, since such is the order of God's Providence. But self-love is not satisfied with this dispensation; it wishes to see, it wishes to know, it wishes to have lights which God is not pleased to give it. As for you, however, be ready, by a complete surrender of yourselves, to embrace every state that it shall please God to send you. Make not the smallest reservation as respects either the nature of these sufferings, their amount, or their duration. A great servant of God desired life only on the same condition on which our Lord received His own, that is, for the purpose of sacrificing it. He even offered himself to God, as ready to suffer to the very end of time; and it seemed to him that there could in this world be nothing to regret save the not being fastened to the cross with Jesus Christ.

We will conclude this chapter with some excellent remarks of a religious of the Order of St. Dominic, in his book "Of The Cross," with reference to the prophet Elias. He considers, then, that this holy patriarch and prophet prepared himself for receiving the sweetest communications from God by suffering heavy crosses; by the withdrawal of sensible graces, and that so complete that he prayed for death, lying prostrate at the foot of a tree in the deepest solitude, for he was all alone in the midst of a desert; by an entire privation of all human aid, expiring of hunger and thirst; by the suspension of all sensible divine succour, being abandoned by God and a prey to the most overwhelming sadness. And then, when he is about to appear before God, we find him still seeking concealment, covering his face under the veil of his mantle in the darkness of his cave; and in this state it is that he is admitted to the sublimest communications from God, a state in which he would seem to be shut out from all knowledge of Him. And thus by the road of abandonment and darkness he arrives at such a wonderful vision of God as he had never been able to attain by all the devotion of his sacrifices and the heroic acts of his religious vocation. Let us learn from this, that the most painful derelictions are in reality the most divine gifts and communications. Let us learn that appreciative love, which is a strong love, the genuine love of friendship and of charity, has so much the more virtue in it the less it is mingled with intentive love, which is a sensible love, a love of tenderness.

CHAPTER IX.

WE OUGHT TO LIVE AS IF THERE WERE BUT GOD ONLY AND OURSELVES IN THE WORLD.

THIS maxim supposes a great truth, which lies at the foundation of all solid perfection; viz., that God is the great All, and that everything else is nothing. A truth very little known, and one that few even of those who know it understand. It is true that many speak of it; it is common enough to hear people say that the whole world is nothing; but as for any practical realization of it, this is far rarer than we imagine, I do not say only amongst people of the world, but even amongst those who pass for being the most spiritually-minded. For where will you find one among those who make the strictest profession of devotion, who has ceased to be jealous about a point of honour, or who no longer cares to be held in esteem by creatures? And if there are persons who find it easy to despise the esteem and friendship of the worldly, where will you meet with those who are perfectly indifferent as to what good people may think of them?   Oh, how much self-love is mingled with the most pious conversations, associations for good works, spiritual friendships and intimacies! Oh, how much gratification does nature find in all these! Where will you meet with a spiritual person, who, like a true Christian, rises superior to all the evils that may befall him from men and devils, earth and hell?

And now, if you seek for the cause of this, you will see that it is the little knowledge they have of the utter nothingness of all things before the All-Adorable Being of God. For how can he who is deeply penetrated with the nothingness of every created being, care for anything belonging to it? How can he love it, and attach himself to it? How can he fear it? Will a reasonable person bestow his esteem or his love on what is nothing? Will he harass and distress himself about what is nothing? Surely this would be absurd. He, then, that acts thus, shows plainly that he is far from having any true and solid knowledge of the nothingness of all things before God, seeing that he is so eager after these things, so grieved at being deprived of them, so full of joy at their possession. O Christian soul! why art thou afflicted at the loss of thy reputation, when it is mangled by the tongues of men and annihilated in their estimation by the ill opinion entertained of thee? Why art thou distressed at the loss of thy goods, or at being deprived of what the world, nature, and sense most covet? Learn once for all, at the foot of the Crucifix, that all honours, all pleasures, all riches are nothing. And why, then, distress thyself about nothing? Learn also that all devils and men together are nothing before God. Why, then, trouble thyself for human respect, and the esteem and friendship of creatures? Why afflict thyself on account of their opposition or desertion? Why disturb thyself at the temptation of devils, since all these things are nothing? I pray our most gracious and most merciful God to fill us with His divine light, for the sake of the Blessed Virgin, all the nine choirs of angels, and the saints, that we may once for all be perfectly convinced of this great truth—that God is all, and that all else is nothing. But those who would learn more on this point I would refer to what we have written in our work on "The Reign of God in Mental Prayer." All that we will here add is, that we must give good heed to be faithful to the light of this truth, when it is granted to us. It is easy, when in prayer we are penetrated with it so strongly that it appears irresistible, to see the utter nothingness of every created being before God; and we can scarcely conceive another state of mind. Fidelity consists in remaining firm in the belief of this truth when the senses powerfully fight against it, and nature rebels, and the mind feels itself moved by the common opinion of men. Then it is that pure faith is the only remedy against all these repugnances, and to its guidance ought we entirely to yield ourselves. Wherefore, although the world may tell us and our senses may make us feel as if pleasures, honours, riches were things of much importance, yet must we, in defiance of our own feelings and the opinions of creatures, adhere closely to faith, which must convince us that God is the Great All, and that all else in His divine presence is nothing. Yes, O my senses—for this ought we to think and to say—yes, O thou world, I see that you would attract me to the esteem, the love, or the fear of created things; but I leave you that

I may follow a divine light, to which I desire unreservedly to adhere, whatever opposition nature and the inferior part of my soul may offer. In fine, let us be assured that this divine light, when it not only enlightens the understanding, but by its heat inflames the will and leads the soul to the practice of virtue, cannot possibly be the result of the efforts of the human mind. It is at the feet of Jesus and Mary that this light is received through the aspirations of holy prayer—sacred exercise, which communicates more solid knowledge to simple women and poor ignorant people, than the deepest study can impart to the most learned and intellectual among men ! It is thus, O my God, that Thou art pleased to bestow Thy purest lights on humble souls, whilst Thou hidest them from the wise and prudent of this world. Ah ! how often does it happen that this preacher or that learned man, after declaring that all things are nothing, is himself very far from practising the truth he announces.

This is not the case with the soul which by self-renunciation and prayer has rendered itself capable of receiving this heavenly light. In an inexplicable manner it discerns everywhere the nothingness of all things. It says with the prophet, "I beheld the earth, and lo! it was void" (Jer. iv. 23), as contrasted with those who behold it full of pleasure and of glory. It is void in its eyes, because it perceives therein neither solid pleasures, nor true riches, nor real greatness. It beholds it as nothingness ; because, the all-gracious God manifesting Himself to it, everything which is not He vanishes in His divine presence. This it is that makes it find deserts in the midst of the most populous cities, whilst sometimes, alas! a religious solitary, who still harbours some esteem for created things, finds a vast world in his little cell. This it is that makes it dwell in a wide and boundless solitude, even in the midst of that society with which in the order of God's providence it is compelled to mix, for everywhere it beholds but God only. Oh, how deeply is a soul which is enlightened, touched at beholding with what the minds and hearts of men are occupied! How is it filled with pity and compassion at seeing them wasting themselves on so many nothings! Its grief is beyond expression when it observes how eagerly they follow, and what a value they set on a fine intellect, brilliant talents, eloquent words, influence with the great, the applause of creatures. It sees clearly that these things, by the ill use that is commonly made of them, are the cause of the greatest evils. Ah! how many religious houses have relaxed in the strict observance of their rule, and contracted a worldly spirit, by allowing themselves to value these things; and so have unhappily led the way to the relaxation of the holiest Orders. What a lesson is here given to all superiors to put their hand resolutely to the work and apply a remedy at once; otherwise they will make themselves responsible for the declension of a whole Order and all the wretched consequences that flow therefrom. O my God, what account will they have to render at Thy tremendous judgment-seat! I warn you, then, that you must not only consider these things as they are in their beginnings, but look to their ultimate effects. A spark is a trifling thing, but unless it be at once extinguished, it may kindle into a flame and cause a terrible conflagration.

"Never turn your eyes away from the Adorable

Jesus," cried the seraphic St. Teresa. And truly, this amiable Saviour is our only model : He sees the whole world in the light in which God sees it, even as a drop of dew, a mere nothing; and thus it is that we ought to regard it. All that passes therein ought to seem to us only as a shadow and a dream. Father De Condren used to call God his world, his sun, his light, his warmth, his country, his father, his life, his repose; in a word, God was all things to him. He treated the world as if he knew it not; and, indeed, as the holiness of God separates Him from all beside, so that He lives and operates only in Himself alone and for Himself alone, so, when He blesses His creatures with a certain participation therein, it produces in them an entire separation from everything that is incompatible with His purity; and this to such a degree that it cannot endure even an attachment to the sensible presence of Jesus, so far as it may be a satisfaction to self-love; Jesus Himself declaring it incompatible with the perfection of His pure love. The Apostles, to whom He announced (John xvi. 7) that He must needs deprive them of His sensible presence, in order to send down upon them His Holy Spirit, whose office it was to establish them in the holiest ways of His love, were imperfect in their affections only by reason of the natural satisfaction which they felt in His presence, and the self-love consequent thereupon. This is why the divine Paul exclaims (2 Cor. v. 16), "Henceforth we know no man according to the flesh; and if we have known Christ according to the flesh, yet now we know Him so no longer :" that is to say, he was dead, not only to all human complacency, but even to such as is divine, so far as it is capable of gratifying self-love.

We may, indeed, then say, that we ought to die to all things, however excellent they may be : to supernatural graces, when self-love mixes itself up therewith ; to the holiest persons, when they tend to turn us from God only. This being so, what can those persons say who try to excuse themselves under the specious pretext of the excellency of the things that occupy them, or of the persons to whom they are most closely attached ? Is there anything more excellent than the sensible presence of Jesus ? is there anything that more closely affects us ? But do we not read that when Moses, in the old law, which was only the shadow and the figure of the law of love under which we live, was called to converse with God on Mount Sinai, he not only separated himself from all the people, but left also his brother Aaron and even Josue, his minister, who was ever with him.

Now the best and the most effectual means of stripping ourselves entirely of all attachments, is to live in the world as if there were but God only and ourselves in it : for what can detain the attention of him who, shutting out from himself the sight of all creatures, has no eyes save to gaze on God alone ? It is impossible to entertain any feeling of complacency, or desire, or craving, or affection for what we have no knowledge of : that which we regard as nothing does not occupy our mind or heart. A mere nothing communicates no impulse to the passions ; it is not capable of exciting in us envy, or anger, or hatred, or sadness, or annoyance, or disquietude, or fear, or grief, or joy, or ambition, or love. "Oh, what purity," exclaims a great servant of God, " to sojourn on the earth and yet behold God only ; to live therein as one unknown, without a thought of what the world says or thinks of us, without a wish to know or be known of any one, either by name, or following, or appearance; to live in the midst of cities and crowds as if we were in a desert!" In this state we have eyes and see not, creatures never appearing otherwise than as nothing to us; we have ears and hear not, by reason of our utter inattention and indifference as to what the world says of us or of others. Our union with God is most intimate, the nothingness of the created being no opposing obstacle thereto, when the soul is divinely penetrated with this truth. The joy which the soul experiences in its superior part is truly wonderful, for it reposes sweetly in its own centre, away from all the trouble and noise and tumult of creatures. Its peace is profound and immutable, for nothing in the world can interfere with it. In this state we are happily delivered from all obstacles that hinder our walking in the holiest ways of pure love. Riches, pleasures, honours no longer have any attraction in our eyes, for, as we have just said, we regard them as nothing. For the same reason we no longer care about dress, or personal adornment, or furniture, or houses, or rich possessions. We easily despise beauty and all natural talents, having no one to please. We are no longer anxious to display ourselves, or to gain the esteem and friendship of men; for it would be simple folly to wish to display ourselves where we no longer perceive a spectator, or to desire the esteem and friendship of that which is nothing. We have no difficulty in enduring contempt and repulse, the grossest insults, the most outrageous calumnies, ingratitude, desertion, the loss of friends and nearest relatives, or of any other persons; poverty and the extremest misery: for the soul, divinely enlightened as to the nothingness of all these things, is neither surprised nor troubled at what, after all, is nothing. Ah! how sweet, how blessed, yea, how divine, it is to live in the world as if there were but God and ourselves.

After all, do as they will, they who are so unhappy as to bestow their esteem and affection on the world and the things of the world must ere long have their eyes opened to the vanity and the nothingness of this same world, its pleasures and its honours; but it will be late indeed, for it is only at the hour of death, when we have no longer the power of remedying the evil, that we fully discover the illusions that have caused us to go astray after creatures. "All will pass away like a dream," said a servant of God; "our ancestors are gone, their very memory has perished; the rise and fall of their fortunes, the pleasures and the pains which once so deeply occupied their hearts, and which they had so much difficulty in reconciling both with the law of Jesus Christ and with the spirit of their times—all is vanished. And may we not rightly esteem them deficient in understanding if they regarded aught else but God in their ways? So also will it be with us—everything will pass away, and God alone will remain. Why should we not do during a few years of a life which quickly passes away what, unless we are lost for ever, we shall do for a whole eternity? For if we attain to heaven, it will be to a place where God alone is all in all. Blessed, a thousand times blessed, that soul to whom God alone suffices in this life, as He suffices in heaven.

CHAPTER X.

WE OUGHT TO HAVE A SPECIAL DEVOTION TO THE HOLY FAMILY OF OUR LORD, TO THE HOLY ANGELS, AND TO ALL THOSE SAINTS WHO HAVE BEEN ESPECIALLY CONNECTED WITH THE HIDDEN LIFE OF THE ADORABLE SAVIOUR.

ALL who have any love for the hidden life ought doubtless to have a special devotion to the Adorable Jesus divinely hidden on this earth of ours, together with the most holy Virgin and the glorious St. Joseph. This Holy Family ought to be the chief occupation of their minds, the subject of their ordinary thoughts, admiration, and love. In whatever state they may be, whether they are engaged in the world, or live in the solitude of cloisters, the Stable of Bethlehem and the House of Nazareth ought to serve as the common retreat of all lovers of the hidden life. Into these sacred places must we at once take our flight, shunning creatures, who try to occupy us with the esteem of created things, and indifferent to what men say or think of us. Ah! what strength will not the soul derive from the sight of the divine mysteries that are being enacted in these holy spots. If it contemplates seriously the complete, the awful privation of all riches, honours, and pleasures which the Adorable Jesus endures, together with His blessed Mother and St. Joseph, can it entertain the least doubt as to the dignity and excellency of such a state? Jesus is God, and consequently He cannot err in His choice of a state of life. Let the world, then, think and say what it will, we must abide by the judgment of a God-Man, and every mind must submit itself to the unfailing and infallible light of Jesus. Never were creatures so much loved by Jesus as were the most pure Virgin and her virginal spouse, St. Joseph: and yet it is these well-beloved of His Heart whom He calls to share most largely with Himself in the privation of those things which the world seeks and loves. It is, then, the greatest favour that He can show us if He admits us to some little participation therein. This being so, how is it possible that we can be grieved by that which ought rather to be matter of the greatest rejoicing to us? Nay, if it be possible to taste innocent pleasures on this earth, we must seek them in the hidden life, and in all its results and accompanying circumstances. Oh, how sweet, with Jesus, and Mary, and Joseph, to have no share in the applause and friendship of creatures, but to be repulsed, forsaken, crucified by them! Let us add, that an interior devotion to these objects of our love, thus divinely separate from the world, fills the soul with heavenly light and strength, so that we are enabled both to discern the excellencies of the hidden life and to enter upon a true and faithful practice of it.

Let us be devout, then, to Jesus hidden; and to this end let us meditate on what has been said in this little work, that we may inflame our hearts more and more with the love of the obscure life of this God-

Man: and this cannot be more fitly accomplished than by conforming our life to the divine life of this amiable Saviour.

Let us be devout to the most blessed Mary, His Virgin Mother, the most hidden of all pure creatures. She was hidden from the very commencement of her most holy life, and, even before she was of an age to appear in the world, by her abode in the Temple. She was hidden when she came forth into the world at the time of her marriage, Divine Providence giving her a poor carpenter for her virginal spouse. Truly, for a daughter of a royal line, this was indeed to be hidden. She was hidden in her divine maternity, although this ineffable prerogative ought to have made her known through the whole habitable world, and to all reasonable creatures on the face of the earth; and, what is altogether wonderful, is that the very thing that ought to have served the most to manifest her, is that which keeps her most concealed. She is so unknown in Bethlehem, that there is not a house that will afford her its meanest apartment for her divine delivery; of all those multitudes there is not one but finds a sheltering roof; it is the Virgin alone who is driven from every door. Had she not been the Mother of God, she would have found room like the rest: but to the Mother of God only a stable will be given, Providence having destined a manger to receive her Divine Son at His birth. And here we may observe by the way, the dealings of God with those who are most dear to Him, and learn what St. Teresa declares she heard uttered by the very mouth of our Lord Himself: that He sends the greatest trials to those whom He loves best. They who do not stand so high in His divine favour have not so large a share in His crosses ; while the consolations of this present life are granted in abundance to His greatest enemies. I leave you to make the reflections which necessarily flow from these great truths. The most holy Virgin is marvellously hidden amidst the idolatrous people of Egypt ; she is hidden after an astonishing manner in the workshop of a poor carpenter ; and again amidst the applauses with which men followed our Lord on account of His miracles : for she uttered not a word, nor did she, as His Mother, draw attention to herself. She listened to His preaching like the most simple of the women who acccompanied Him ; and it is even related (Mark iii. 31) that, while our Lord was preaching, she stood at the door without, saying not a single word to gain admittance, but waiting there like the meanest in the crowd. She was hidden at the foot of the cross, sharing in all the shame and all the ignominy of her well-beloved Son. We may, indeed, say, and be lost in an abyss of admiration at the thought, that her love for the hidden life was wonderful beyond measure. This truth is made evident beyond all power of expression by the amazing silence she maintained towards St. Joseph, though she saw him grievously troubled on account of her divine pregnancy ; for may we not truly marvel at her silence, when by a few words she might have relieved him of all his anxiety ? When, too, we consider that St. Joseph was her husband, that he was grieved on her account, and that she entertained for him the deepest love which in the order of God one creature could feel for another ? She sought concealment even when manifested in the most holy manner : witness her conduct when, St. Elizabeth greeting her with a thousand benedictions and praises, she took none of them to herself, but referred all to God. She kept herself hidden by leading a poor and abject life, dressing herself most simply, never wearing gay apparel, and gaining a hard livelihood by sewing and spinning. Nay further: she desired to hide her immaculate purity, hesitating not to appear as though unclean on the day of her most holy Purification. She desired to pass for a sinner—she who is purer than the sun and the very angels themselves. In fine, she hid herself from herself, never preferring herself to any creature in the world, as St. Mechtilde says she learned by divine revelation : thus in all companies she took the last place, as saints have observed in reference to what is related by St. Luke in the Acts of the Apostles (i. 14). And, to say all in one word, never was pure creature more hidden, seeing that it is God alone who really knows her, and who alone, as the Fathers declare, comprehends all her grandeurs and perfections.

Let us be devout to St. Joseph, who, next to Jesus and Mary, was most hidden. Every one is aware how little we know of the admirable acts of this incomparable saint. You might, indeed, say that Jesus takes delight in making him the most hidden of men, suffering him to die before His own public life began, in which this holy man might have had some share, and have performed acts which might have given the sacred writers occasion to make mention of him. Oh, how ought conduct like this to convince us more and more of the greatness of the hidden life ! Certainly we may truly say that it contains excellencies beyond all thought, since Jesus loved it so deeply and so tenderly, and chose it for those whom it was His will to raise to the highest rank in eternal glory. Is it not a mark of predestination to a high and incomparable glory in heaven, when the whole life on earth is a hidden one? We just now beheld what bore the semblance of unkindness towards St. Joseph in the heart of the most tender of creatures, the virginal heart of Mary, in that she concealed from him in his affliction the mystery of the Incarnation; let us now consider the also seemingly harsh conduct of Jesus towards this most admirable of saints. It is Jesus who is the master of life and of death. St. Joseph therefore dies because it is His pleasure He should die. It is Jesus, then, who banishes him from His presence, and at the same time separates him from his virginal spouse. Consider by the way that it was to inflict a grievous sorrow on His most holy Mother, thus depriving her of the greatest consolation which in this world she could derive from a pure creature; and consider herein the manner in which God treats His dearest favourites. But further, in removing Joseph from His presence, Jesus sends him to the prison of Limbo, and that for several years. If, then, you pay attention to all the circumstances of our Lord's dealings with St. Joseph, you will see that Jesus mortified him in the most astonishing manner; and hence you will learn that the benefit of mortification is exceedingly great beyond the power of words to express. Ah! can you ever again complain of your interior pains, and of the withdrawal of the sensible presence of God from your soul? Some one may say that our Lord sent St. Joseph to Limbo, to announce His coming to the holy Fathers who were detained therein. This is true, but He might have done all this by the holy angels. In short, He desired that St. Joseph should be wholly hidden.

Let us be devout to the great St. John the Baptist, whose life was hidden in so extraordinary a manner, because God desired to exalt him to an extraordinary sanctity. Let us be devout to St. Mary Magdalene, who spent so many years in a solitary cave; to St. Paul the Hermit, St. Onuphrius, St. Alexis, St. John Calybite, and all the saints who led a solitary and retired life. But let us not forget the saints who, distinguished in the world by the exalted offices they held, led nevertheless a hidden life by the ignominies they endured, the slanders and calumnies with which they were defamed, the contempt and scorn with which they were treated, being known among men only to be accounted the offscouring of the world. Such were the glorious Apostles St. Peter, St. Paul, St. John the Evangelist, and the other Apostles and disciples of our Lord. And through all ages you will see, following their steps, a long train of saints who were truly admirable in this kind of hidden life; for, as was said above, these abasements keep those who suffer them more closely concealed amidst cities and crowds than are hermits in their solitude.

Bear in mind also the holy angels who appeared to the shepherds, and sang in the heavens above them, at the birth of the Son God. Remember him who revealed to St. Joseph the mystery of the Incarnation; and him who announced the flight of our Lord into Egypt, and, again, His return into Galilee; those, too, who served our gracious Saviour in the stable of Bethlehem, and in His exile in Egypt, and during all His hidden life at Nazareth. Be mindful of the holy angels who attended on His most holy Mother; the blessed angel-guardian of St. Joseph, and all the blessed angel-guardians of those saints whose life was hidden, either in an exterior solitude, or by the ignominious crosses they endured. We may say that these blessed spirits demand especial veneration from all who are devoted to the hidden life, seeing they have assisted so powerfully in ministering to it. Assuredly devotion to these glorious beings is one of the great means by which we can enter upon this holy practice; and the aid we receive from these spirits of pure love is so great that words are too weak to express how greatly we ought to love them. If you would learn the way, you may study it in a little book which our Lord and His Blessed Mother gave me grace to compose in their honour, entitled, " Devotion to the Nine Choirs of the Holy Angels." God only, God only, God only.

A PRAYER TO THE HOLY SPIRIT.

HOLY SPIRIT, my God, lost in the abyss of my own nothingness, in Thy presence, who art infinitely adorable, I implore the continual assistance of Thy exceeding goodness, and the succour of Thy great mercy, for myself, a wretched sinner, who desire to exist only for Thy glory, to do nothing save for Thy sacred interests, to live only of Thy pure love.   Ah ! my God, cast me not away from Thy presence, withdraw not Thyself from my soul : according to the multitude of Thy mercies, be Thou the Spirit of my spirit, the Soul of my soul, the Heart of my heart ; henceforth let me be nothing to myself or to any other creature ; let me be wholly Thine, solely Thine, universally Thine, without the smallest reservation, that Thou alone mayest reign in all I am, and in all I do, and shall do for ever.   Amen.   Amen.   Amen.

A PRAYER TO THE MOST HOLY MOTHER OF GOD.

O HOLY VIRGIN, worthy of all veneration, Mother of grace and mercy, prostrate at thy sacred feet, in all humility I beg thy holy blessing. Bless me, O my most sweet, most gracious, and most faithful Mother, whose precious and divine Heart alone contains more kindness, more sweetness, more tenderness, than all the hearts of all earthly mothers united.   Bless this little work, wholly dedicated and consecrated to the holy hidden life which thou didst lead here below on earth with the All-Amiable Jesus and the glorious St. Joseph, thy virginal spouse. Bless all those who shall read this work, and for it, and for its readers, and for its author, obtain the benediction of thy gracious Son, our great and only All, our Adorable Saviour and our God. Obtain from the Holy Spirit those divine lights which enlighten our understandings and inflame our wills, that we may know the excellencies of the hidden life, and love it, and truly practise it, so far as the designs of God in our regard require of us ; that, being hidden from the world, we may lead a life wholly of grace, wholly superhuman, wholly spiritual, in intimate union with the Amiable Jesus, and acting only by the movements of the Holy Spirit, to whom alone, with the Father and the Son, be all honour and glory world without end. Amen. Amen. Amen.

THE END.